OPTIONS TRADING
FOR BEGINNERS

An Updated 360 Step by Step Guide on How to Trade with Options Starting From the Basic Jargon to a Critical Fundamental and Technical Analysis.

HENRY LIVING

Copyright - 2020 -

All rights reserved.

The content contained within this book may not be reproduced, duplicated or transmitted without direct written permission from the author or the publisher.

Under no circumstances will any blame or legal responsibility be held against the publisher, or author, for any damages, reparation, or monetary loss due to the information contained within this book. Either directly or indirectly.

Legal Notice:

This book is copyright protected. This book is only for personal use. You cannot amend, distribute, sell, use, quote or paraphrase any part, or the content within this book, without the consent of the author or publisher.

Disclaimer Notice:

Please note the information contained within this document is for educational and entertainment purposes only. All effort has been executed to present accurate, up to date, and reliable, complete information. No warranties of any kind are declared or implied. Readers acknowledge that the author is not engaging in the rendering of legal, financial, medical or professional advice. The content within this book has been derived from various sources. Please consult a licensed professional before attempting any techniques outlined in this book.

By reading this document, the reader agrees that under no circumstances is the author responsible for any losses, direct or indirect, which are incurred as a result of the use of information contained within this document, including, but not limited to, - errors, omissions, or inaccuracies.

Table of Contents

INTRODUCTION	5
CHAPTER 1 UNDERSTANDING OPTIONS	7
CHAPTER 2 DIFFERENT TYPES OF OPTIONS	49
CHAPTER 3 LEARN ABOUT OPTIONS PRICING	61
CHAPTER 4 WORKING WITH CALL AND PUT OPTIONS	77
CHAPTER 5 START TRADING OPTIONS PROFITABLY IN THE MARKET – HERE'S HOW	87
CHAPTER 6 CREATING YOUR TRADING SYSTEM	95
CHAPTER 7 GETTING STARTED	103
CHAPTER 8 THE ROLE PLAYED BY OPTIONS EXCHANGES	111
CHAPTER 9 THE OPTIONS TRADER MINDSET AND PSYCHOLOGY	117
CHAPTER 10 OPTIONS TRADING SOFTWARE	135

CHAPTER 11
HOW TO PLACE AN ORDER 143

CHAPTER 12
HOW TO CLOSE AN OPEN CALL OR PUT OPTION BEFORE EXPIRATION DATE 155

CHAPTER 13
PLATFORMS AND TOOLS FOR OPTIONS TRADING 159

CHAPTER 14
RISK MANAGEMENT IN OPTION TRADING 173

CHAPTER 15
TOP MISTAKES TO BE AVOIDED BY NEW OPTION TRADERS 207

CHAPTER 16
TIPS TO HELP YOU SUCCEED WITH OPTIONS TRADING 219

CONCLUSION 235

Introduction

This is a step-by-step guide that will help you understand options with relative ease, and it will teach you how to make smart trades and win consistently.

The following chapters will discuss all that you need to learn about options. This includes options trading, options contracts, charts, and the different types of options available. Options trading provides traders with a realistic chance of becoming wealthy. There are plenty of millionaires in America and elsewhere who have made their fortunes trading stock options.

But the pursuit of this additional income should never be reckless or at all costs. Apart from the investment being carefully considered, you should always have backup funds in case anything goes wrong. And anything can go wrong. From incorrect information to unforeseeable external factors that no one can ever think of and plan against. This does NOT mean that it will go wrong.

Therefore, you should only go for options trading if you have funds to spare after having covered your basic expenses like the everyday food on the table, the utility bills, the loan repayments, and the sort. Any venture of this kind should be considered as a means to acquire funds for future events that will require great amounts of money, like putting the children through college and not as a means of acquiring access to fast profits and luxuries.

It may very well provide you with the means for such amenities. But it should never be the initial objective. It should be a fortunate byproduct. Options trading is an investment just like any other investment and is therefore supposed to work for the future.

Chapter 1

UNDERSTANDING OPTIONS

WHAT ARE OPTIONS?

Before we get into some of the strategies that you can use for options trading, you must take a look at options and know what they're about. Many parts come with options and there are many choices that you can make with this kind of trading. You need to understand how these options work at their most basic level. Options can be complicated and understanding the basics can make it a little bit easier for you down the road. Let's take a look at these options and what they are so we can start investing in them today!

If you were to find an investor and ask to look at their portfolio, you will be able to see that they have a large variety of investments that they are working on. They don't just put all their money on one company all the time.

An option is a contract that gives the investor the authority to purchase or sell an asset or a security, such as a stock or a bond. This is like getting a key where once you use that key to open the front door of a house, then it belongs to you. You may not technically own the house because you have the key, but you can use that key whenever you would like and if you choose, you could purchase the house later on.

Now, several methods will work when you are dealing with options. Some of the ones that you will come across regularly include:

BONDS

A bond is a debt investment where the investor can loan out their money to the government or company. Then this money will be used for a variety of projects by the second party. But at some time, usually determined when the money is given over, the money will be paid back along with some interest. Most of the time you will work with a government bond and these bonds are even found on the public exchange.

COMMODITY

Commodities are another choice that you can make when you are working with options. These will be any basic goods that will be used in commerce and can include some choices like beef, oil, and grain. When you trade these, there will be a minimum of quality that they must meet. These are popular because commodities are considered tangible, which means that they represent something real.

CURRENCY

Currency is any type of money that is accepted by the government and can include coins and paper money. Of course, cryptocurrency and Bitcoin are starting to join the market as well. The exchange rate of these currencies, especially when it comes to digital currencies, will change quite a bit in very little time so you must be careful with these.

FUTURES

These are similar to what you found with commodities, but they have some different guidelines on how they can be delivered, the quantity and quality, and more. Both parties on this one will need to fulfill their end of the contract to make it work. A futures option is a contract that will allow one person to buy or sell an asset at the futures price, but at a later time, though they can decide not to purchase as well.

INDEX

An index is a group of securities that are imaginary and will symbolize the statistical measurement of how those will do in the market. These aren't tangible at all and it gives you the right to sell or buy the value of the index at the exercise price before they expire.

STOCK

Stocks represent a certain number of shares in a company. You can own a certain percentage of the share, but instead of running that company, you will let other management do that while you make some profits each quarter when the company does well.

HOW OPTIONS WORK?

You will find that these options work differently than other investment options you worked with in the past. These options are contracts and they are also price probabilities of events that may or may not happen in the future. If something seems as if it is likely to happen, then the option will be more expensive than one that is less likely to happen. Understanding how these options work will make it easier for you to pick out an option that will make you the most money for its value.

Let's take a look at an example of how this could work by using a call option with IBM. The strike price is $200 with IBM currently trading at $127 and the options will expire in three months. Remember, the call option will give you the right (although you won't be obligated), to purchase shares of IBM at $200 anytime during the next three months.

With this option, if the stock prices of IBM end up going above $200, you will win. It doesn't matter that we aren't sure of the price for this particular option right now. What we do know is that this option, if it expires in one month rather than three months, will end up costing less because the chances of anything occurring during this smaller interval of time is smaller. On the other hand, if this same option lasts for the next year, it will cost you more because it is more likely the stock price will go up to $200 or higher sometime during that year.

Let's bring it back to the three-month expiration that we started with. Another thing that will make it more likely that you will win in this option is if the price of this stock does get closer to $200. The closer that the stock price is at the beginning, the more likely that the event you want will happen. As the price of your asset rises, the price of the call option premium will rise as well, but as the price goes down, the gap between the strike price and the asset price will widen and the option will start costing less. For example, if you set the strike price at $190 instead of $200, your cost for the option will be higher because it is more likely that the stock will reach $190 instead of the higher price. If the strike price is $230, your options price will be worth less because it is less likely that the option will get that high.

WHEN SHOULD YOU USE OPTIONS?

As an investor, you will have several opportunities to use options. However, there are a number that are truly beneficial. Here is a brief look at them.

- Options buy you time if you need to sit back and watch things develop
- You require very little funds to invest in options compared to buying shares
- Options will offer you protection from losses because they lock in price but without the obligation to buy

Always keep in mind that options offer no free ride or a free lunch. Trading in options carries some risks due to their predictive nature. Any prediction will turn out one way or another. The good news here is that any losses that you incur will only be equivalent to the cost of setting up the option. This cost is significantly lower than buying the underlying security.

BASIC VOCABULARY FOR OPTIONS

Okay, so let's get some jargon out of the way so that you can navigate the options markets and understand what people are talking about. We have already mentioned a few of the terms, but let's review them right now.

STRIKE PRICE

If an option is exercised, shares are traded at the strike price. So, this is the price per share that the shares of stock would be sold to a buyer if we are talking about a call option. If instead, it's a put option, this is the price per share that the trader who sold to open the contract agrees to pay to purchase the shares from the buyer of an option. The strike price is set when the contract is opened and is good until the option expires.

EXPIRATION DATE

Every option comes with an expiration date. When trading options, it's important to know when the expiration date is. If you are only trading options with no intent to exercise them, you don't want to ever be stuck with an option on the expiration day. Options typically expire on Fridays, but for heavily traded options on exchange-traded funds, they expire Monday, Wednesday, and Friday. A "standard" option is one that lasts a month. These options will expire on a Friday. It will be the third week of the month, but some options only last for one week (called "weeklies") and there are also options that last several weeks to two years. An option that lasts for more than a year is called "LEAPS" which means Long-term Equity Appreciation Security. There is nothing special about them other than the expiration date, otherwise, they are just like other options.

TIME DECAY

Since something that expires has less value the less time there is available on the contract, options suffer from a problem called "time decay". Options get some of the pricing from "extrinsic" or "time" value. The smaller the amount of time remaining on the contract, the lower the time value. If the stock is moving in a favorable direction, however, the value of the option that is related to the current market cost of the stock and a couple of other factors can overwhelm time decay.

To know what the time decay is, you can look up a quantity called theta that will be listed for every option. It will tell you how much the option price will drop at the market open the following day. So, if an option has a theta of -0.11, that means that it's going to drop in price by 100 shares x $0.11 = $11 at the next market open. This may or may not be important. Other factors can swamp that $11 and make it irrelevant. But you need to be aware of it.

IN THE MONEY

If the strike price is favorably positioned concerning current market prices, it is known by this term. For a call option, it will be in the money if the share price (on the market) of the stock is greater than the price known as the strike price. For a put option, it will be in the money if the price that would be paid for the stock just buying it is less than the strike price. When an option is in the money, its value has heavily influenced the price that the stock is trading at. In the ideal situation, which can happen as an in the money call option approaches expiration, a $1 increase in the stock price will translate into a $100 change in the price of the option that would go up as well. Of course, this cuts both ways, so it can mean a $100 loss if the share price is moving the other way.

AT THE MONEY

If the strike price is the same as the share price on the market, it is known by this phrase. At the money, options can offer a relatively low priced way to enter a trade and take advantage of the movements in share price that are likely to make it go in the money if you have done your homework and entered a good trade.

OUT OF THE MONEY

For a call option, it's said to be in this state if the strike price is greater than the market price. If the option expires out of the money, it is said to expire worthlessly. For a put option, it will be out of the money if the share price is above the strike price.

PUT OPTION

a put option is an option contract to sell a particular stock under the terms of the put option contract. With a put option, you are 'putting it into the ownership' of the option buyer.

CALL OPTION

a call option is a contract to buy a stock according to the terms of the call option contract. A call option means you are calling upon the seller to sell you the stock, at the contract terms.

WRITER

a writer is an investor who sells an option, like a call or a put.

HOLDER

a holder is someone who buys an option, i.e., holds the option.

BID PRICE

a writer buys at the bid price, and the holder sells at the bid price. Think of the writer as 'bidding' to buy the option at the bid price.

ASK PRICE

a writer sells at the asking price and a holder buys at the asking price. Think of the writer 'asking' the asking price to sell an option.

INSIDER TRADING

Insider Trading is both tempting and illegal, in most countries. Insider Trading consists of making investment decisions based on information not available to the general public. If you act on information you read in the Wall Street Journal, that is not insider trading. If you act on information from your neighbor, who is a top-level executive at the company, that is insider trading and is illegal.

LEVERAGE

Options trading gives you the chance to buy options for a whole lot less money than buying the underlying stock. Your dollar goes further trading options than by trading stocks and for a given amount of money you invest, you can control many more shares with options than you can with buying the stock itself.

WASTING ASSET

A wasting asset is one that declines in value over time. For options, the rate of decline becomes very rapid as the option approaches the expiration date. Of course, on the expiration date, the option's value goes to zero. This is the extrinsic value and is related to the time value of money.

LEAPS

LEAPS is the acronym for Long-term Equity Anticipation Securities. LEAPS mostly behave just like all other options but instead of having an expiration date of a few weeks or months, LEAPS have a lifetime of one or more years. This longer lifetime tends to smooth out the effects of volatility and allows, with the same leverage as regular options, the benefit of the longer-term performance of the underlying security. LEAPS are available for most commonly traded equity stocks and equity indexes like the S&P 500.

OPEN INTEREST

This represents the total number of option contracts open at the time, whether they are puts or calls.

AMERICAN OPTION

an American option is an option, whether a put or a call, that can be exercised at any time before the expiration date. American options are usually sold on the stock market.

EUROPEAN OPTION

a European option can only be exercised on the expiration date, not before. However, it can be sold before the expiration date. European options are generally sold on the "Over The Counter" or OTC market.

BUYER AND SELLER

for every purchase or sale, there must be a sale or purchase that corresponds with it. The table below describes that correspondence for the buyer and seller. Notice that the buyer has the option but not the obligation to act, whereas the seller must act if the buyer chooses to execute the option. Here, we refer in the most general sense to an investment 'instrument' which could be a common stock or, for example, an ETF.

	BUYER	SELLER
CALL OPTION	Right to buy the particular instrument	Obligation to sell the particular instrument
PUT OPTION	Right to sell the particular instrument	Obligation to buy the particular instrument

EXECUTE

This means that the buyer decides to act on the contract, to buy or sell; that is to execute the contract. It is also referred to as Exercising the Option.

EXPIRATION DATE

when the contract is agreed upon, it runs for some finite period. After the expiration date, the contract expires; that is it is no longer valid. After the expiration date, the value of the option is zero.

STRIKE PRICE

the strike price is the stock price agreed to in the put or call option contract. For example, if you were to buy a call contract for Google (GOOG) at $695, that means you have the right but not the obligation to buy 100 shares of Google stock at $695. That is the strike price. It is also called the Exercise Price. Similarly, a put option for GOOG will have a strike price.

ASSIGNMENT

to be assigned means that an option you hold has experienced some event that requires you to respond. Reaching the expiration date with a stock put option that is in the money requires you to deliver the stock.

MARKET PRICE

the market price is the current price of that stock today. Market prices vary minute by minute on the stock exchange.

OPTION PREMIUM

there is a cost for buying an options contract, either put or call. That charge, collected by the seller, depends on the length of the contract and the practice of the broker. Premiums can range from a few cents per contract to closer to $20. Option premiums are paid in cash, the cash you have in your brokerage account.

INTRINSIC VALUE

Value of the premium derived from the value of the underlying stock.

EXTRINSIC VALUE

A portion of the premium related to volatility and time.

COMMISSION

a buyer of an option has to pay the broker to carry out that purchase or sale, just as she has to pay a commission for the sale or purchase of any stock or other instrument.

UNDERSTANDING OPTION CONTRACT

An option contract has three elements to it: the strike price, the option type, and the expiry date. The strike price is not to be confused with the option contract price. The strike is simply the level beyond which the option comes 'into the money'. This is best explained via an example.

If you buy a call option for a stock, say AAPL, with a strike price of $160, this means you can buy the underlying stock at any time before its expiry. Since you've bought a call option, ideally you want the stock's market price to be greater than the strike price. This way, you can buy the stock at the lower option strike price and sell it at the higher market price. Thus, the call option is in the money in such a scenario.

For a put, on the other hand, you can only make money when the underlying market price is lower than the option's strike price. So, if you purchased an AAPL put with a strike price of $160, you can only make money when the stock is trading for less than $160. It is only in this scenario that the put is in the money. Hence, the strike price is the price which the market price must cross, the direction depends on whether the option is a call or a put, for you to make money on the option.

Next up is the expiry date. Options contracts don't exist forever, they expire at certain periods. The most common expiry date for an option is the last trading day of a month. Options usually exist for month-long periods although there are some cases where they may exist for longer periods, sometimes years. These longer options are called LEAPS and are not the subject of our discussion in this book.

When you pull up quotes for an options contract in your broker's terminal, you will usually see contracts for three expiry dates: the current month, the next month (near month), and the month after that (the far month). Trading volumes are the greatest for current and near month options, with near month volumes gradually increasing as the current month's expiry date draws closer.

As the name, expiry date, suggests, the contract is not valid beyond this date and must be exercised either on or before this date. This brings us to the type of option. There are two types available: American and European. American options are more widely available and are preferred as trading instruments because they can be exercised on any day before the expiry date.

By contrast, European options can be exercised only on the expiry date and not prior, and not after. As you can imagine, this isn't very ideal for a trader since your chances of being right are greater over some time, like with the American option, as opposed to a day.

The next thing you ought to familiarize yourself with is the option contract ticker. The ticker for a contract is an amalgam of information so let's break this down. I'm going to use an actual example here.

AAPL190607C00150000 is an option that is currently trading at $25.60 with a strike price of 150 and expiring on June 7th. This is a call option. Here's how this is broken down:

AAPL-this is the underlying stock's symbol, in this case, Apple Inc.

190607-this is the expiry date listed in yy/mm/dd format. Hence, June 7th, 2019.

C-This indicates this is a call option. A put would be denoted by a P.

00150000-This is the strike price represented as five digits before the decimal and three after. In this case, it is 00150.000 or $150.

Similarly, AAPL190607P00145000 is a put option on AAPL, expiring on 7th June 2019, with a strike price of $145.

Options are generally a lot different compared to most other financial securities like stocks, commodities, bonds, and currencies. The value of an options contract depends upon the value of the underlying asset. As such, options are ideally contracts permitting future transactions based on the underlying security. The contract is entered by two parties consisting of a buyer and a seller.

The contracts come with terms relevant to future transactions. For instance, there is always a definition of the underlying asset and its properties.

For instance, the contract will define the underlying security, the price, expiration date, and if it can be sold or purchased.

Investors have plenty of financial and strategic leeway with options compared to simply investing in stocks. By investing in options, traders not only hedge to protect against losses but also gain access to stocks at a fraction of the normal costs. Options contracts lower your risk in all market conditions on speculative bets and increase your profits on any new or existing positions you may take.

Trading in options has a lot of positives compared to trading in stocks only or other securities. However, there are some inherent risks that you need to be aware of. As a potential trader, you need to be aware of the great benefits as well as inherent risks relating to trading options.

There are various standardized components of option contracting that enable ease in engaging in options trading. These components characterize the mechanics of how options trading binds the parties involved and demonstrates the way profits can be generated if the market forces are favorable.

AMONG THE COMPONENTS OF OPTIONS TRADING ARE:

UNDERLYING SECURITIES

Options that are traded on the market only apply to certain assets. These assets are then referred to as underlying securities. The word shares can be replaced with the word shares in certain instances. Some companies provide the asset against which the option operators list options. ASX is one operator in the options trading market has played a key role in the listing of underlying securities.

The term classes of options refer to the listing of puts and calls as options of the same assets. As an example, is when puts and calls are applied to a lease corporation's shares. This does not put in regarding the contract terms in terms of the predetermined price or duration of the expiry of the call and put contracts. An operator of options trading usually provides the list of the available classes for the benefit of investors.

CONTRACT SIZE

On the ASX platform of options trading, the market standardizes the size of the option contract at 100 underlying securities. One option contract, therefore, corresponds to 100 underlying shares. The changes that can happen only come when reorganization happens on the initial outlay of the underlying share or the capital therein. Index options usually fix the value of the contract at a certain stipulated dollar rate.

EXPIRY DAY

Options are constrained by time and have a life span. There are predetermined expiry deadlines that the platform operator sets which have to be respected. These deadlines are usually rigid, and once they are out the rights under a contract in a particular class of unexercised options are then forfeited. Usually, the last day of the life span of a contract is the summative trading date. For shares that have their expiry coming by June of 2020, the options over them have their last trading day on a Thursday that comes before the last Friday that happens to be in the month. Those that expire beyond June 2020, expiry is on the third Thursday that happens to be in the month. For index options. Expiries come on the concurrent third Thursday of the same month of writing the option. However, these dates can be readjusted by the options platform operator as and when there is a reason for such action.

In recent years, platform operators have introduced more short-term options for some underlying. Some are weekly, while others are on a fortnightly basis. These have the corresponding weekly or fortnightly expiries. When the lifespan of options runs out, the operators then create new deadlines. However, all classes of options have their expiries subject to quarters of the financial calendar.

EXERCISE PRICES

These are the buying price or the price of selling the assets or underlying securities. These prices are also called strike prices. They are usually predetermined in the option contract and have to be met if one has to exercise the rights in an option. Essentially, they are called exercise because the parties are now invoking the rights that are stipulated in an option either to buy or sell. The exercise of the option is, therefore, subject to the price stipulations.

The prices are usually predetermined by the platform operator. Various prices can be listed as available on the market for the same expiry of a certain class of options. Usually, prices depend on the value of the underlying share value. If the value of the underlying prices increases, the exercise prices also increase commensurately. The need to offer a range of prices for the same option contract is to suit the market conveniences of buyers of the contracts. The buyer can better match their expectations of the pricing of the underlying shares given the position of their option contract. The exercise prices can also be varied in the course of an active contract when market dynamics dictate that such a move has to be made.

ADJUSTMENTS TO OPTION CONTRACTS

There is a general effort to ensure that option contracts are entered under conditions that are standardized to the greatest extent possible. However, some market forces may upset the set optimum conditions and specifications. This may call for the making of some adjustments to ensure the preservation of the value attached to the positions of the various options contracts that have been entered into by various takers and writers.

In making the adjustments, it has to be established the kind of upset that has been caused on the market.

Usually, it may affect one or more components of the options market. Identifying the affected components is necessary so that the adjustment is specific and particular to the kind of area of trading affected.

ASX, as one of the platform operators, has its rules that try to retain a tentatively predictable and standardized environment of trade. However, it also provides guidelines for the kind of measures that have to be made when adjustments are required. Conventions that guide the process of adjustment cushion participants on this kind of market and also protect takers and writers from arbitrary actions that may be unfavorable.

PROS OF TRADING OPTIONS

YOU REQUIRE MUCH LOWER UPFRONT FINANCIAL RESOURCES THAN WITH STOCKS.

The cost of buying options, which includes the premium amount and trading commission, is much lower compared to the amount you will pay to invest directly in shares.

As an investor or trader, you will pay far less money to invest in the same number of shares compared to one who invests directly in shares. However, if the trade is successful, then you will benefit just as much as a direct investor percentage-wise.

LIMITED LOSSES WHEN YOU INVEST IN STOCKS AND OPTIONS.

When you purchase stock options, you are not required to exercise your right to buy or sell the underlying stock. If your estimations or speculation about the stock movement are right, then you make a large profit. However, should your speculations not follow through, and then your losses are limited only to the cost of the premium and brokerage fees.

OPTIONS OFFER TRADER'S FLEXIBILITY ON THEIR TRADES.

There are a couple of strategies that can be implemented by investors or traders before the expiry of the contract. Here are some of these strategies:

- You can exercise an option and purchase the underlying stocks then add these to the portfolio.

- You can also exercise an option contract, purchase shares, and then sell them for a profit at the stock market.

- You can make back some funds that were spent buying an out-of-the-money option. This is by selling the option to another trader before it expires.

- You can also exercise options that are in-the-money to other investors.

LIMIT YOUR RISK

Some people are scared of ever getting into the derivatives trading market, lamenting that it is a very risky pursuit, but that's not the case. Of course, there are instances when options can be risky, yet there are also situations wherein options can help you minimize risk. It all comes down to how you utilize them. Options take less financial commitment than equities, and they are also resistant to the negative effects of gap openings.

COST EFFICIENCY

The leveraging power of options is great. Thus, a trader may acquire an option position similar to a stock position, but at a significantly lower price. With options trading, it is possible to make great profits without necessarily having large amounts of money. Individuals that operate on a tight budget have found options trading very accommodating. A shrewd trader can employ leverage to increase their trading power without necessarily injecting more capital.

BETTER LEVERAGE FOR THE MONEY

When working with options, it can provide you with some good leveraging power. A trader will be able to buy an option position that will imitate their stock position quite a bit, but it will end up saving them a lot of money in the process.

FLEXIBILITY AND VERSATILITY

Another benefit of options is the flexibility that they offer. For instance, if your investment approach is to buy and hold, you will simply buy stocks either for the long term or short term. The long-term stocks should appreciate over time and the short-term stocks should perform faster for regular dividends. The investment strategy of buying stocks doesn't confer to investors avenues of risk limitation or strategies of increasing their earning potential.

HELPS TO HEDGE INTRADAY OR FUTURES TRADES

It is common for traders to purchase or short-sell Futures contracts because they expect them to move in one direction or another. Intraday traders may do the same thing because they will purchase a large number of shares in the hopes that they will move down or up during that day. If the trader ends up picking the wrong direction on the Futures or the intraday trades, they may end up losing a lot of weight. Unless you put in a stop-loss, you can lose an unlimited amount of money in the process.

OPTIONS CAN HELP YOU TO FIX THE STOCK PRICE.

Option contracts act similarly to lay-away in stores because they let investors fix the price of a stock at a specific value which in our case is the strike price for a couple of days, weeks, or months. This guarantees you that an investor will be able to sell or purchase the underlying security at the strike price before the option expires.

POTENTIAL FOR ASTRONOMICAL PROFITS

One of the main reasons for trading options is the opportunity of making significantly large profits compared to all other forms of trade in the markets. This is possible even without large sums of money. The principle behind this approach is leverage. A trader need not have large amounts of funds to earn huge profits. For instance, with as little as $10,000, it is possible to earn amounts such as $300,000 or even $800,000 simply by using leverage.

GREAT RISK VS. REWARD CONSIDERATION

Like all good traders, it is essential to weigh the risk posed by a certain trade compared to the possible rewards. When trading using options, then the style adapted will indicate the type of risk inherent in the trade. The above example clearly shows how profitable options trading is. If a loss was to be incurred in the above instance, then the total loss would have been the cost of the options.

VERSATILITY AND FLEXIBILITY

Another extremely appealing benefit of trading in options is the inherent flexibility. Options offer lots of flexibility with dozens of different strategies to pursue. This compares well with numerous other trade and investment options out there. Most of these do not offer as much flexibility as options do. Also, most other securities have limited strategies, and this tends to limit the flexibility that a trader has on that security.

CONS OF TRADING OPTIONS

While options have certain amazing benefits including flexibility, they do carry some disadvantages. Traders must understand the risks and cons associated with trading options. The numerous benefits have seen more and more traders, including amateurs and pros, venture into the world of options in the hope of cashing in on this lucrative trade.

NOT AN EASY TASK

First of all, it is advisable to note that trading options is not as simple as it sounds. Options are complex securities. They are contracts that come with certain terms. These terms need to be clearly understood and taken into consideration at all times. Part of the options contracts has to do with time. Unlike stocks and other securities, options have a time limit. This time decay factor makes them extremely short-lived. If a trading strategy does not work out, then the options could expire and be worthless.

TRADING OPTIONS IS A RISKY VENTURE

The options trading process is considered an extremely risky affair. All investment opportunities and even trading ventures carry a certain element of risk. The traders most at risk are beginners and novices. These groups are generally not as well versed or sufficiently experienced to deal with options. Knowledge is crucial in options trade but experience is essential. Rather than hemorrhage money, traders prefer to avoid options trading altogether.

TAX

Except for extremely rare instances, all your gains are taxed as income. This is the same as taxing your income because the tax rates levied upon your gains are just as high. One clever way investors can step around the taxation issue is to utilize their tax-deferred accounts such as the IRA. Sadly, not everyone has ownership of a tax-deferred account. The tax can reduce the amount of money you take home, but considering the high earning potential, options are still profitable.

COMMISSIONS

In comparison to stock investing, commissions for options are significantly higher. For most active traders, their annual commissions usually exceed 30% of the total amount you invested. To guard yourself against paying exorbitant commissions, never sign up with a broker without being clear. Whenever you receive a newsletter, quickly check to see the commission details. Options trades will cost you more in commission for every dollar that you put down. The commissions may even be more for spreads that require you to pay commissions for both sides. A trader should be careful about the broker that they choose to work with. For instance, if you're a beginner, you should stick to brokers who cater to beginners.

TIME VALUE DECAY

In stock trading, you can purchase long-term stocks that can take decades to mature. But options contracts come with an expiration date. You can't stop the process of expiring. Also, the option's position relative to the date of expiration affects the premium that you will pay to acquire the option. The more the options get closer to the expiration date, the more the rate of time value decay increases. Therefore, monitor your open positions so that your options don't expire worthlessly.

UNCERTAINTY OF GAINS

Investors try to minimize risk by examining the risk profile graphs. This shows them the projected gains or losses at the next expiration of options contracts. In as much as these graphs are helpful, especially when placing the initial position, they still cannot guarantee you a profit. It can be hard to project the gains from an options trade. Sometimes, after the expiration of options contracts, the expected gains are not generated. But there are other times when, at the expiration of options contracts, the earnings exceed the projected gains. In that sense, your gains or losses become somewhat uncertain—terrible for individuals who loathe uncertainty.

REGULATION

One of the things that bother traders and investors is the regulations imposed by governing bodies. The OCC, Securities, and Exchange Commission (SEC), or even the court has the power to impose restrictions on exercising various options. Although it rarely happens, it is still enough of a concern that it can make traders think again before putting down their resources into acquiring options contracts. You should always perform your due diligence over the underlying assets that you intend to take options contracts for. If the assets are at the center of legal battles, you might want to take a pass.

LOWER LIQUIDITY

A lot of individual stock options don't have much volume. If it is not among the most popular stocks or indexes, the option you're trading is likely to be low-volume because each stock will have a different strike price and expiration. You must note that the liquidity issue only becomes a huge factor if the trades are big-money. In the case of a small trader who purchases around 10 options contracts, liquidity is never going to be an issue.

COMPLICATED

It's not beginners alone who can get overwhelmed in the world of options trading. Some professional traders seem to think that they understand options trading when they don't. To understand options trading, you have to dedicate a significant amount of time to study all the aspects of this field. As a beginner, the worst mistake you can commit is to sign up with a broker that caters to professional traders. You have to look for a broker that caters to beginners so that you could utilize their educational resources. There's so much to learn before anyone could become proficient in options trading.

LEVERAGE

Leverage is most dangerous when you're selling naked

options or entering into unlimited-risk strategies. Options trading affords investors many trading tools. The tools can make or break you. It is upon the investor to use these trading tools for their benefit. The biggest step an investor can take for success in options trading is to first acquire the requisite knowledge. Guesswork is bound to get you into major losses.

SELLERS ARE EXPOSED TO LARGE AND SOMETIMES UNLIMITED LOSSES

Option buyers and holders are only exposed to small losses. However, the option writer's risk is almost unlimited. The losses that they stand to incur are so much greater than the cost of the options contract. The reason is that they have obligations of purchasing or selling stocks or the underlying stocks if a buyer or seller chooses to exercise their right.

TIME IS ALWAYS LIMITED FOR THE INVESTOR TO MAKE A PROFIT

Options are short-term in nature. Investors who use options often seek short-term or near-term price movements that they can capitalize on. These price movements need to take place within a matter of a couple of days, weeks, or months for the payoff to happen.

TRADERS HAVE TO QUALIFY TO TRADE

As an options trader, there are certain essential criteria that you must meet if you are to start trading.

For instance, you must be approved by a broker. You do this by answering a couple of questions or going through a similar screening process. The broker will need to find out about your financial situation and your knowledge and experience with risk and understanding of how to trade options.

OPTIONS TRADERS CAN INCUR ADDED COSTS THAT AFFECT RETURNS

Certain strategies need you to set up a margin account. For instance, when you are selling a call options contract on securities that you do not own. This margin account provides a line of credit that is held as collateral in the event the trade moves against you.

AMERICAN VS. EUROPEAN OPTIONS STYLES

AMERICAN STYLE OPTIONS

When it comes to trading options, we have two distinct options styles. These are European style options and American style options. American style options refer to the terms of an options contract. It does not necessarily refer to the country or continent where the sale took place.

Each option contract comes with certain features including an expiration date. It is upon this expiration date that the buyer gets to exercise their right to purchase the underlying stocks. In the case of a put option then the buyer will reserve his right to sell the underlying security.

The distinction between the two comes in here. When it comes to American stock options, the contract owner or buyer has the right to exercise it at any time. The contract does not have to expire for rights to be enjoyed. This type of contract is extremely flexible and provides traders with many benefits and opportunities which they can rightfully exercise.

EUROPEAN STYLE OPTIONS

European stock options are similar to all other options. The only challenge is that they are not as flexible. The American style options are flexible because they allow the buyer or holder leeway to lay claim to the underlying stock/ the European style contracts accord rights to a buyer but these rights are only exercised upon expiration of the contract between seller and buyer. The rights cannot be exercised or enjoyed before the expiration date.

Traders will only be able to enjoy their rights upon the expiration of the contracts. At such points, they may choose to exercise their rights or forfeit them. Most options contracts are of this kind. Many that are traded across the world are of this nature where parties have to wait a couple of days or weeks until the contract is about to expire.

TRADING LEVELS

Before you start thinking about trading options, you need to be aware that brokerages classify options traders by level. Since options trading is a bit tricky and carries some risk, brokerages don't just allow you to do anything up-front. The level you are assigned determines what types of trades you are allowed to take part in. Specific details may vary from broker to broker, but they tend to follow the same rules.

LEVEL 1 TRADING

The first level is very restrictive, in fact, it only allows you to sell to open options contracts under strict conditions. In the first case, you can do what is known as a covered call. This means you will sell a call option that is covered, meaning it is backed by 100 shares of stock. In other words, you have to own the shares of stock before you can sell a covered call. As we will see, many people who own shares of stock use covered calls to earn monthly income from their investments.

Level 1 traders can also sell to open a protected put. A protected put is an option that is backed by the cash needed to buy the shares of stock should the option get exercised. While a protected put has the benefit of providing financial security should the option be exercised, it requires a large amount of capital in your account. It turns out there are other ways to sell puts with relatively low risk, so it's hard to imagine many people selling protected puts.

Level 1 options traders cannot buy options, and they cannot trade options (that is buy an option, and then sell it for a profit).

LEVEL 2 TRADING

A level 2 trader can sell covered calls and protected puts. Also, a level 2 trader can buy calls and puts and trade them on the market. Level 2 traders cannot engage in advanced trading techniques like spreads. Moreover, they are not officially allowed to enter into strangles and straddles, although they can do them indirectly by purchasing options on an individual basis.

Most readers are probably hoping to be at least a level 2 trader. Becoming a level 2 trader requires you to submit to an interview process by the broker. The good news is that the "interview" is done via computer these days, and it is pretty easy to get approval as long as you know what to say. The two main things you need to be aware of before undergoing the interview is that the broker will want to know your investment goals and time horizons. Your answers will need to assure the broker that you understand how options work.

Firstly, they will ask you if your goals are long-term capital appreciation or short-term profits. Even if you have a stock portfolio or IRA you are managing for your retirement, you need to tell the broker your investment goal is to make short term profits. Secondly, they will ask if you are interested in speculating or investing. You need to tell them that you are interested in speculating. That means that you are buying financial securities with the hopes of selling them for a profit in

1 year or less. Again, what your real goals are overall is not important - you need to tell the broker what they want to hear if you are planning on trading options.

LEVEL 3 TRADING

If you have not done any options trading, you are probably going to have to spend a few months at level 2 and buy and sell some options before you are approved for level 3. Level 3 opens up some new possibilities for you. As a level 3 trader, most brokerages will allow you to engage in certain options strategies that help minimize risk and increase the odds of profit. You will be able to sell options even without cash or owning the stock – as part of one of the pre-defined strategies. The strategies that level 3 traders can use include credit and debit spreads, straddles, strangles, and more complicated trades like an iron condor. Some of these strategies involve the simultaneous sale and purchase of options, and they can even involve call and put options simultaneously. Many brokers set them up for you and will give you the estimated profit and loss in each case.

LEVEL 4 TRADING

Level 4 is the highest trading level at most brokerages. This allows you to engage in any type of options trading, including selling "naked". This means that you can sell options that are not backed by any cash or collateral. However, that is not strictly accurate, as brokerages require a margin account to engage in that type of trading. To open a margin account, you must deposit $2,000 cash. Then, the broker uses a formula to determine the fraction of capital you must have in your account to cover a trade. Keep in mind the money is never spent, it is kept in the account as insurance. While a "protected put" might require you to put $10,000 in your account, for a "naked put" you might only need $1,500. The specifics depend on the specific strike price, underlying stock, and other conditions.

Level 4 traders also have access to more advanced trading strategies. These include using multiple legs and special strategies such as a "butterfly" or iron butterfly.

Each additional level of trading gives access to anything a lower level trader can do, so a level 3 trader also has the powers of a level 1 and level 2 trader. For junior traders, it is best to trade some options straightforwardly at level 2, before moving up to advanced levels.

OPTIONS TRADING FOR BEGINNERS

One of the benefits of new traders who decide on options trading is the adaptability that this kind of speculation is putting forth. Amateurs may have the chance to trade with influence. In individual nations, an option contract might speak to 100 offers of the underlying stock or ware. The traders don't need to set up the majority of the capital for the hidden resources however they deal with a small amount that speaks to the whole sum that is identical to the estimation of the stocks or the items. This influence allows the traders to control a large volume of the primary resources through options contracts.

In any case, although fledgling traders have the focal points realized by adaptability and influence, they must be cautious as options trading presents high dangers. Traders might deal with little measures of investments; nevertheless, they can bring about gigantic misfortunes simultaneously if they are not cautious. To reduce the risks associated with this kind of trading, new traders need to utilize strategies. They may, for instance, use Option Combination. They can buy or sell different options contracts all the while. There are additionally different strategies that they use to acquire instead of losing.

While fledgling traders learn the nuts and bolts of buying and selling options contracts, they additionally need to learn progressively about the necessary resources that they are dealing with. They must know about the components that may impact market costs and patterns. Traders ought to have the option to change their position as needs are. They may ensure their job, or they may receive in return contingent upon the market circumstance. New traders must be cautious in settling on choices particularly when an excess of hypothesis impacts them.

Options trading is a hazardous business, and this may not be for everybody. The individuals who might want to give their hands a shot need to wander with a hazard capital. The general idea of this sort of trading increases the hazard that traders are taking. Learner traders additionally need to find out about it if they choose to put resources into options. Right working information about techniques and strategies will be useful to tenderfoot traders with the goal that they may not wind up in a weak position. There are lots of subtleties and data about options trading, and there are likewise experts who can give sound advice to the individuals who are new to this sort of trading.

MAKING MORE OF YOUR MONEY

Options trading is an investment vehicle for experienced investors, who track their investments proactively. It's anything but a reasonable car for investors hoping to keep up assets without direct administration, as it's mainly a planning-related buy and buoy. Options trading is an astounding strategy for utilizing money related influence to make more fabulous buys.

Options trading has its arrangement of phrasing, which we'll get into somewhat later, yet the essential reason is this: You buy an option to buy a stock or ware at a given value; the option lapses after a given timespan (American style options trading), or the choice must be practiced on a particular date (European style options trading).

There are two standard sorts of options that are traded. Calls increase in an incentive as the stock cost rises, and places increase in an excuse as the stock cost decreases. (There's a lot of financial arithmetic behind both of these. However, the layman's clarification will do the trick.) In many cases, options are sold to different investors just before they lapse; most options traders don't finish up holding partakes in the stock they have options for; the possibilities are purchased, sold, exchanged, and executed before their termination dates. It is conceivable to have both call and put options on a similar item or stock; this is a "straddle" methodology.

Options trading is undoubtedly not an easygoing investment methodology; it's a technique utilized by individuals who are contributing as their calling, or who plan to deal with their very own wealth straightforwardly. The advantages of options trading are adaptability, coupled with (on account of put options) somewhat of a countercyclical system for bear markets.

Options exchange is a lower chance procedure done by floor traders and can be short term benefits, with significant liquidity. The point is to swap options with different traders before specific elements impact the market, or to dispose of failing to meet expectations options while still getting some benefit out of them. Options exchange is maybe the best spot to begin in options trading for a beginner.

MANUAL FOR OPTIONS TRADING FOR BEGINNERS

Options are considered as subordinates as these budgetary exchanges depend on the estimation of assets or underlying securities. In contrast to stocks, options lapse on specific dates and they have no predefined fixed number with regards to its accessibility. A great many people may not by any means see how options work yet some of them have been utilizing it in their trading business. Fledglings need to comprehend that there are two sorts of options that they can chip away at. The first is the call option where they can buy a stock for instance at a given cost before a predetermined date for example. This may be compared to buying security deposits.

Traders pay for the option premium when they buy call options. This installment gives them the privilege to buy the underlying asset at a pre-decided strike cost later on. Traders may not obtain the stock for instance since they are not obliged to do as such but rather all the while, they will have lost money as far as the option premium if they mostly sit tight for it to terminate. The second kind of option that they can execute with is known as the put option. Traders can sell the underlying asset at a cost concurred and at a predetermined date. Place options for this situation might be compared to protection strategies.

Traders can practice their put option, and they can sell the asset at a projected cost. When the price of the underlying asset goes up, they don't have to practice their put option and their sole expense caused is the premium. The call and the put options are utilized by traders to reduce the hazard that they are taking. The individuals who buy options are given the privilege to work out. Traders who might want to practice their call option may buy the underlying security at the given strike cost, and the individuals who might want to exercise their put option may sell it at a price settled upon.

Although call and put traders are given the privilege to buy or to sell, they are not obliged to do as such. They may choose to practice their rights relying upon their investigation of the market. There are various ways for traders to sell their options besides exercising their rights. They may exchange through shutting a buy or a sell, or they may essentially select relinquishment. Traders may desert their choices if the top-notch that is left is lesser than the expense of exchanging it.

Chapter 2
DIFFERENT TYPES OF OPTIONS

There are generally two major classes of options. These are put options and call options. Like previously defined, put options give you, the investor, an opportunity to sell stocks at a specified price while call options give you the option to buy stocks at a certain price.

UNDERLYING ASSET

Every option contract is based on an underlying asset. Most options are based on stocks of companies that are listed in the stock market. In recent years though, other securities have been used. These include REITs or real estate investment trusts, ETFs, or electronically traded funds, foreign currencies, and stock indices. Some are even based on commodities like minerals, industrial, and agricultural products.

Stock options contracts are generally based on 100 shares of the underlying stock. Some exceptions are made in special cases for instance where mergers occur or when there is a stock split. Also, buying options is completely different to investing in shares. Here is a look at different types of options.

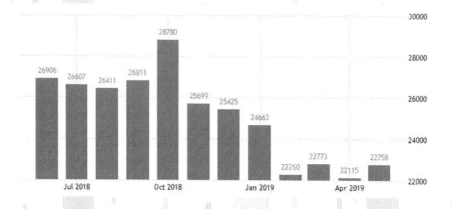

DIFFERENT TYPES OF OPTIONS

NEAR MONTH IN-THE-MONEY OPTIONS

Some options are best suited for day trading. One such example is the near month in-the-month option.

This option refers to options contracts that are set to expire at the close of the next month. Such options are usually past their strike price so investors are free to exercise them.

The inherent value of this options contract is one of the determining factors of the premium especially when it nears its expiration date. Such options are often traded in large volumes and this causes a smaller gap between the asking and bidding prices. As the option nears its expiration date, its time value diminishes.

PROTECTIVE PUT OPTION

A protective put is an option that is used by traders who wish to purchase both an option and its underlying securities. This is the preferred strategy anytime that the underlying stock is expected to undergo periods of high volatility.

There are instances when day traders will continually buy and sell the same stock option for a long time, maybe a couple of months, to benefit from a short term upward trend. At other times, day traders make use of a strategy of purchasing put options on the same underlying security just so they insure themselves against any sharp losses in the stock's price. This is considered as a risk management technique. While there are certain small losses paid to protect the share, the opportunity to minimize losses on a downward trend is invaluable.

STOCK OPTIONS

Traders acquire a way to increase their profits through straightforward stock options by simply purchasing or shorting shares at a certain set price at a set date at the options market. Day traders have certain advantages when it comes to stock options because the parameters are applied to stock options. Since both stock options and stocks are traded on an exchange, the market will have the same liquidity and will enable the fast execution of orders. Sophisticated investors can use options as an effective hedge against risks.

Stock options have the potential to cost you 100% of your funds. Brokers only permit sophisticated traders to deal in complex options systems like stock options. You can be exposed to enormous amounts of risk and you must avoid strategies that require substantial experience. But it is good to note that day traders rarely sell options.

WEEKLY OPTIONS

Weekly options are also popularly referred to as weeklies. Such options are generally listed with only one week left to expiration. Most options often have several months and sometimes even years to expiration. However, weeklies are generally available to day traders. They are found on ETNs or exchange-traded notes, broad-market indices in the US, and ETFs or exchange-traded funds.

A lot of traders view traditional options as a huge setback largely because of the long time duration. These traders very much prefer weeklies and view them as major game-changers. They get to apply the leverage of options even as they engage in more short-term strategies.

CREATED ON THURSDAYS

Weekly contracts are usually created once each week on a Thursday. They remain valid until the following Friday for ETNs, ETFs, and equities. Weekly index options, however, often close their final trading sessions on Fridays or Thursdays depending on the index. These have a total lifetime of seven trading days or one week.

As a day trader, you can benefit hugely if you take advantage of the increased volatility that comes with the time decay and expiration that is associated with options. Weekly options have 52 expiration periods throughout the year and this increases your chances of benefiting from expiring options.

While weeklies provide a couple of advantages to day traders, they have some possible disadvantages especially due to time factors. Option buyers generally pay a lower price for the cost of a weekly option compared to regular options. They usually experience a hugely limited opportunity window, especially when trades move in the opposite of the intended direction. There is generally a very limited opportunity for the price to recover and it is hard to fix a trade through strike adjustments.

MINI OPTIONS

Mini options are options that let traders and investors trade in options that are based on 10-share sets rather than the standard 100-share sets. Mini options have expiration dates that are similar to regular expiration dates. This expiration date is also similar to quarterlies and weeklies.

Other features like the bids, strike price, and offers are also similar and correspond to features of regular options. However, they do offer certain benefits. As a trader, you stand to enjoy the following benefits by simply trading in mini options.

INDEX OPTIONS

We also have another type of options contract which is known as the index option. These options let you make use of put or call options to speculate on the movements of a whole stock market index like the S&P 500 or the Dow Jones instead of individual stocks and shares.

A trader who trades index options can capitalize on their predictions based on volatility or direction of an entire market without any need to trade options based on individual stocks. One of the main challenges that traders encounter when pricing index options is accurately calculating dividend estimates.

BINARY OPTIONS

Binary options are among the most commonly traded options. They are known by different names depending on the platform where they are trading. For instance, binary options are referred to as FROs or fixed return options when traded on the American Stock Exchange. On the Forex markets, they are referred to as digital options and sometimes as all-or-nothing options on the ASE or American Stock Exchange.

The reason why they are known as binary is that this options class offers returns or profits in two outcomes. This means you get something or nothing. In this instance where you have binary options, the profitability is usually a pre-set amount such as $100. Certain assets can be traded as binary options. These assets include;

- Stocks
- Commodities
- Currencies
- Stock indices
- While there are plenty of different types of binary options, only two are commonly used by day traders. These popular binary options are;
- Asset or nothing binary options
- Cash or nothing binary options

The asset or nothing binary option pays the entire value of the underlying security. The cash or nothing binary option pays an investor a set amount of money should the option be in-the-money upon expiry. This is the reason why this type of option is referred to as binary. You can expect to receive only one of two outcomes investing in this particular options class.

The reasoning behind binary options day trading is pretty simple. As a trader, the aim is to enter a trade position and exit before the close of the trading day. All binary options contracts come with expiry times and dates. This means that most binary options contracts have a set expiry date except on trading platforms where traders have variable expiry on options.

As a day trader, you should identify expiry dates that will conclude trades within the same day. This is because once you enter a trade that has an expiry date, you will not be able to exit manually the same way that you do with all other options trades.

FUTURES OPTIONS

Options on futures are contracts that are focused on one futures contract. As a buyer, you reserve the right to choose a futures position on an index, currency, commodity, or other financial prices. The options trade is at a specified price known as the strike price and you maintain your right until the expiration of the option.

A future options seller is obligated by the contract to assume the reverse futures position as soon as you exercise your right. These options trades are dealt with on the same exchanges with traditional futures contracts. The options contracts concisely match the underlying securities, which in this case are futures contracts. The matching is in terms of the strike price, expiration dates, and quantities.

There are certain differences between futures and options futures. As an example, buyers and sellers have different obligations. It is advisable to find out more about the differences between options on futures contracts and futures contracts.

ETF OPTIONS

An ETF option is an options contract that is derived from the ETF or exchange-traded fund. ETFs are investment pools that are then traded at the stock market. Electronically traded funds contain a specific number of underlying assets that include bonds, commodities, and stocks. They trade very near to the net asset value throughout the trading day.

The shares and other financial instruments are traded in much the same manner as for regular stocks at the bourse. This way, a trader is easily able to purchase and sell shares and even options of an electronically traded fund via a brokerage account. You will find ETFs across all the common stock indexes such as the Nasdaq 100 composite (QQQQ) and the Dow Jones Industrial Average. Sometimes traders will choose a specific industry because chances are high of finding stocks of major industries across most ETFs. This way, traders can focus more on determining and predicting movements in a specific industry rather than a mixed choice of stocks as offered by standard index ETFs.

ETF options come in very handy as their related options trade throughout the day. As a day trader, if you actively trade ETF options and make use of hedging strategies, then you need to ensure that you are well informed regarding the background information of the underlying stock. If you feel confident about this information then you will gain from the tax breaks and low costs associated with trading ETF options.

IRA OR INDIVIDUAL RETIREMENT ACCOUNTS OPTIONS

Yet another option account that is out there is the IRA options contract. However, IRA accounts are generally unavailable to the general population because of rules put in place by the SEC or US Securities and Exchange Commission.

The SEC demands that any day trader have the appropriate designation and should hold margin brokerage accounts. However, this is not the case when it comes to an IRA account. Such accounts cannot be margin accounts and are limited to only cash accounts.

In simple terms, day trading of stock options and stocks needs traders to operate a margin account and any IRA account used should have only a cash account status. The only alternative that you can have is to create your own IRA account via a commodity futures broker.

OPTION TRADING FOR BEGINNERS

Chapter 3
LEARN ABOUT OPTIONS PRICING

Another useful aspect of options trading that you need to be familiar with is the aspect of pricing options. The option price is also known as the option premium and consists of two distinct components. These are the intrinsic value and extrinsic value. Both are governed by the put-call parity principle.

HOW TO PRICE OPTIONS

Another factor that you need to be conversant with is how to price an option. You must be able to price options correctly and accurately so that you do not incur unnecessary losses. The first step in pricing options is to understand all the elements that are involved.

The pricing process is a science and not an art. Once you master this science, you will be able to price options quite easily. Options prices are determined by numerous external factors. However, 90% of the time, the price is influenced by volatility, stock price, and time till expiration.

FACTORS TO CONSIDER INCLUDE:

STOCK PRICE

When pricing options, the first place to begin is the market price of the underlying security. The security could be an index, a stock, or even ETF or electronically traded fund. This price is the predominant factor in determining the price of a stock.

Imagine Apple's stock trading at $500. The company then introduces a new gadget in the market. This new product is even greater than current gadgets like the iPhone. The shares then gain value and tend towards $550. In such an instance, a lot of shareholders will want to secure exclusive rights to buy the shares at $520. Basically, as the price of the shares goes up so do the call prices.

TIME

Options are a factor of time. This means that they are wasting assets. In other words, their benefits are limited within a certain stipulated period. This could be three months or six months. As an option approaches its expiration date, there is less time to benefit from it. As such, its value decreases proportionately. You must always factor in time when pricing options.

BID AND ASK PRICE

Another crucial factor that plays an important part in option pricing is the bid or ask price. Each option, regardless of whether it is a call or put, always has a bid and ask price.

Basically, when buying options, you will purchase at the asking price or very close to it and sell on the bid or very near to it. For instance, if you are looking at September 75 calls and notice prices like $9.60 x $9.90 then the asking price you'd be purchasing at is $9.90 while the selling price on this option has its lower margins at $9.60. The difference between these two prices is that the asking price and bid price is known as the spread. If the spread is very tight, then it means that the stock is very liquid.

VOLATILITY

Yet another important factor that determines the price of an option is its volatility. Volatility is the most crucial factor in the stock price. Any options that are based on very long-term stable stocks will be predictably priced compared to options whose stocks have hugely volatile charts. Apart from past performance, implied volatility is also crucial so all these factors are considered when pricing a stock.

HOW TO READ OPTIONS QUOTES

One of the best sources for options quotes is the CBOE or the Chicago Board Options Exchange. If you visit the relevant website at cboe.com, you will come across the free twenty-minute delayed screen. However, for a small fee, you will receive real-time streaming quotes and general real-time quotes.

OPTION VOLUME AND OPEN INTEREST

Two crucial pieces of options items that are related can be found marked on the quote. Volume refers to the total amount of trading activity recorded daily for a particular call or put option. Therefore, when a trader is buying or selling options, these will be recorded as part of the day's volumes. Volumes begin each day at zero and keep rising throughout the trading day.

Open interest is a rolling tally of all the open and active options contracts at each strike. The number represents a total tally of all open and unexercised options. This figure does not necessarily change in the day but adjusts itself overnight as soon as all exited positions are closed, and the day's trades are tallied.

One challenge presented by the open interest is that it can remain unchanged or change just slightly. Some traders blame this on day traders who enter and exit positions. However, others think it's because options keep changing hands from one trader to another throughout the day. In any case, traders should always be on the lookout for open interest and daily volume patterns.

EXPIRATION CYCLES

Any time that you are checking out securities with traded options, you are likely to note the different expiration dates as well as the changing patterns from one stock to another. As soon as a particular security begins to trade, it receives one of three random expiration cycles. This is simply because there are numerous other securities trading at the markets that it would be a huge challenge to keep track of each call and put options at every strike price every month.

The three cycles commonly attached to options are:

- January, April, July, and October
- February, May, August, and November
- March, June, September, and December

The most crucial aspect to keep in mind is that there will always be options in the current month and options for the next month. An exception can only occur if a security is delisted from the exchange. Let us assume it is the month of May, and you wish to trade in company ABC's options. You will simply take a look at the May options and those available in the

June series.

You should also take a look at the options chain. This chain is available through your preferred broker. Remember that a chain lists options and the essential details of each option. You can also find the options chain on page one of Yahoo! and even Google. If you closely examine the top of such a chart, then you will note that there are options for May, June, July, and October.

EXPIRATION DATES

You will also be expected to be on the lookout for options expiration dates. The benefit of trading options is that the aim is to trade and profit as fast as possible then exit a position. Profiting within a relatively short period and taking advantage of volatility is therefore quite common.

Ideally, options should expire each month on the third Saturday. However, since markets are not open on Saturdays, the expiry is moved to the third Friday of each month. Therefore, if you purchase an option in July, then you can hold onto it until the third Friday of the month. Beyond this date, the option will not be profitable.

Within the relevant period of your option, you are free to trade your option. You can, for instance, exercise your right to purchase the underlying stock or perform any other activity permissible with options.

FACTORS INFLUENCING PRICES OF OPTIONS

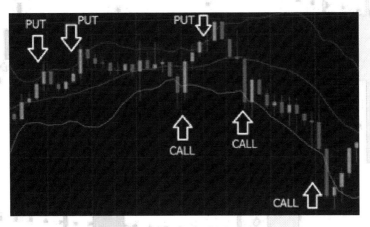

There are many options strategies, but they all arise from two basic options: the call and the put. The put grants the holder the right to sell the underlying security at the strike price before the contract expires. If the stock price is greater than the strike price when the contract expires, the contract is considered to have zero value and would thus expire worthlessly. A call entitles the holder to buy the underlying at the strike price before the contract expires. If the strike price is more than the stock price at the date of expiration, then the option expires as worthless (Folger, 2012).

In both puts and calls, the market maker or investor receives a premium. The premium is the fee of acquiring an option. Here are some of the factors that affect the price of an option:

PROBABILITY

The chance that an option will end up in the money is the main aspect influencing an option's worth. The closer the probability that the underlying asset will end up in the money gets to 100%, the greater the worth of the option becomes; the further away the probability that the underlying asset will finish in the money gets from 100%, the lower the value of the option. As a trader, you have to sharpen your analytical skills and determine whether an option is worthy of the premium it demands.

STOCK PRICE

If you want to acquire an option that entitles you to buy a stock at $50 per share, the premium would be affected by how close the stock price is to the $50, i.e., you would pay more if the stock was trading at $45 as opposed to $40. The higher the stock price, the higher the premium of call options. In the same vein, the lower the stock price, the higher the premium of put options. If you want to sell an underlying at $30, you will pay more for the put option when the strike is at $28 as opposed to $35.

TIME TO EXPIRATION

When there's a lot of time left for the options contract to expire, chances are high that the price of the underlying asset will undergo significant changes. Thus, the premium will be high. On the other hand, as the expiration approaches, the chances of significant change in the price of underlying assets tend to diminish, thus lowering the premium. The date of expiration causes options to have a definitive nature. Thus, if the price of an option seems unbearable, you might consider waiting for the period of expiration to come.

VOLATILITY

This is the measure of how swiftly and extensively the price of an underlying asset jumps up and down. Generally, the most profitable options contracts are volatile. The more frequent and extensive the oscillations, the more likely the option's price will go up. Even the slightest change in the estimated volatility can have a large impact on the premium. A shrewd trader should take the time to research the financial securities that are significantly volatile so that they can maximize their earning potential. The price oscillations of an underlying asset in the recent past are used to determine the premium. If the market takes over and the oscillations happen from moment to moment, then you have a case of implied volatility.

INTEREST RATES

You must note that rates of interest have a slight effect on the value of an option. When the rates of interest increase, the worth of the call will go up, and the put option will go down. The adjustments in the premiums are triggered by the costs of owning the underlying assets. When a trader acquires an options contract, the extra cash can attract interest. A high interest translates into bigger earnings. Therefore, traders are willing to pay higher premiums to own call options.

DIVIDENDS

When a trader fails to receive their dividend, the stock will go down by that amount. A dividends increment causes a rise in the value of both calls and puts.

NATURAL LOGARITHM

The Black-Scholes calculation of premiums utilizes the natural logarithm. The changes in the price of underlying assets are proportional to the price of the underlying.

NORMAL DISTRIBUTION

The normal probability distribution is used in the calculation of an options price. In the Black-Scholes model, price movement is understood to be distributed normally. Small movements have a high probability, whereas large movements have low probability.

NEWS

It seems that financial news plays a critical role in driving the whole derivatives markets. Although chances of it happening are rare, influential finance journalists could drive an agenda that could trigger oscillations in the price of options contracts. But the real captains of the industry are the brokers and market makers. These people who are in charge of brokerages and market-making corporations have the power to influence the course of the derivatives market. When they appear on the news, traders and investors hang on their every word and traders could go on a spree of buying or selling, which affects the value of options.

CROWD PSYCHOLOGY

If there's a sector that asks for mental maturity and discipline, it's the derivatives market. You have to have a plan and know when to take action as opposed to guessing your way around. But people are still people. It's so easy to get distracted by the trends and lose sight of your trading strategy. For instance, if a certain clique of traders reaps sudden profits, everyone runs into their niche in the hope of reaping quick benefits, thus driving the premium of the option up.

PRICE OF THE UNDERLYING ASSET

While they often will not move at the same speed or for the same amounts, an option is always going to follow the lead of its underlying asset. As such, you can always expect the price of related calls to increase along with rising asset prices; while puts will always decrease and vice versa.

TIME VALUE

The amount of time that an option has until it expires is directly related to how likely that same option will ultimately end in a profit greater than the intrinsic value before things are said and done. To determine the amount of time value that the option you are considering currently offers you will want to find the current price of the option and subtract from it the amount of intrinsic value that the same option currently has. It is common for options to hold onto 70 percent of their total value, or more, during the first half of their life before losing value much more rapidly after that point. It is also important to note that time value can change dramatically based on the volatility of the underlying asset both in the moment and based on its expectations in the future. As a general rule, the lower the time value, the more stable the option is likely to be.

INTRINSIC VALUE

The amount of value that an option will hold onto, even at the very end of its lifespan, is known as the intrinsic value. When working with a call option you can find the intrinsic value by taking the current price of the underlying asset and dividing that by the difference between the strike price and the current price. When it comes to finding the intrinsic value of a put option, the process is mostly the same; to start, you subtract the amount the underlying asset is currently worth from its strike price before dividing that number by the current stock price.

The results of this equation will provide you with a clearer idea of the type of advantage that choosing to exercise the option at the moment would provide you with. This number can also be thought of as the minimum that the option will ever be worth, even at the moment of its expiration.

CALCULATING INTRINSIC VALUE

To obtain the intrinsic value of a call option, you will simply deduct the call option's strike price from the stock's actual price or its prevailing market price.

Call Option Intrinsic Value = Stock (share) Price − Call Option Strike Price

An example:

Let us say that company ABC's stock is trading at $450, and its October $400 call option is asking for $50. The intrinsic value, in this case, is calculated by subtracting the call option strike price from the prevailing market price

$450 - $400 = $50.

In our case above, the intrinsic value of the call option is $50. Should this value be negative, it simply means that the call option has no intrinsic value and a put option has no extrinsic value.

EXTRINSIC VALUE

Extrinsic value can also be defined as the premium or time value of a put option. It is the part of the price that is determined by all other factors except for the value of the stock. The extrinsic value is the payment that you are making to the option seller to compensate for the risk that he or she takes for trading the options contract.

The money you are paying the trader or seller is referred to as risk money. The amount paid to the seller is considered justified and is essentially determined by several factors. These factors include dividends payable, volatility, interest rates, and expiration dates.

You will need a pricing model such as the Black-Scholes model if you wish to accurately determine the extrinsic value of any stock option, especially a put option. A stock's price is made up only of its extrinsic value if there is no intrinsic value built into it.

STRIKE PRICE

The strike price is a major component of any options contract. It also happens to be the sole static variable that affects an option's pricing. Each stock that can constitute an option has a different strike price and expiration date.

The strike price is typically determined using the stock's current market price. Take the example of a stock that is trading between $5 and $25. In this case, the strike price will vary with increments of about $2.50. The variations will be, for instance, $5, $10, $7.50, and so on. Let us assume that the stock price is trading between $25 and $200. In this instance, the strike price will progress in increments of $25, $35, $40, or basically in increments of $5.

A strike price of any option is among the most basic determinants of the specific option that you will pick for trading purposes. For instance, if IBM stock is trading at $550 and has a good chance of rising beyond $570 in the coming months. In this instance, you may consider purchasing a $600 call option that has an expiration date of at least two or even more months.

Now when holding this option, you will have the right to purchase IBM shares at $600 even as other purchases at prevailing market rates. This is because the option contract that you hold has effectively secured you the right to purchase at the said price.

Chapter 4
WORKING WITH CALL AND PUT OPTIONS

WHAT ARE CALL OPTIONS?

Call options are options contracts agreed between a buyer and a seller. The seller usually holds certain securities such as stocks, bonds, currencies, and so on. The buyer usually wants to have some form of leverage including buying or benefiting directly from the security held by the seller.

An options writer will write the contract and sell it at a price. This price ranges from $0.5 to $5 depending on the value of the underlying stocks. This amount is paid upfront by the buyer and is non-refundable. The options writer gets to keep this amount as their reward. A trader who buys an option simply earns the right to buy or sell the underlying asset. However, there is no obligation to do so. The contract has a definite expiry date while the underlying security has a predetermined price. A call option generally gives the buyer the right to purchase the underlying security.

WHAT ARE PUT OPTIONS?

Put options are option contracts where a seller agrees with a buyer concerning an underlying asset. In this instance, the seller must sell the security should the buyer choose to exercise their right.

Put options happen to be the complete opposite of call options. The buyer in this instance gets the right to sell the underlying security. The seller on the other hand is obligated to purchase the stocks without the chance to opt-out. Both put and call options have an expiration date. The underlying security determines the price of the option, but other factors are also considered.

HOW CALL AND PUT OPTIONS WORK

When it comes to options contracts, the crucial part in the determination of future prices. It all comes down to probability which means the likelihood of a particular event to occur. For instance, in our airline hedging example, a future price had to be determined. The price had everything to do with probability.

How likely is it that fuel prices will go up in the coming weeks or months? Based on the probability of outcomes, the price can then be determined. We can as well use a call option for instance. The value of such an option goes up with the value of the underlying stock. This is where the relative value of an option comes in. Options are more valuable the more time they have. When they approach expiration, they lose value pretty fast until they become worthless.

Options do not just diversify your portfolio, but they also provide you with immense opportunities of earning large profits with minimal income. Before you can begin trading options, you need to understand the process of buying and selling. You also need to learn how to read tables where options and quotes are printed. There are symbols used when quoting options and tables that consist of a complex array of numbers.

A lot of traders, both small and large, prefer options trading to grow their wealth and benefit from higher profits. This is achievable with relatively small amounts of funds. The profits earned via options are disproportionately large compared to the investments made. One benefit of this type of trading is that you can begin small and grow large very fast. With amounts as little as $80, a small retail trader can invest in options and see gains very soon.

PROBABILITY

Option trading is a very versatile process. This opens up a whole new world of opportunities. You could use options basically to trade and earn profits, for leverage, and also as insurance or protection against potential losses. All of these can be attained conveniently and very quickly.

Because trading in options is a very powerful process, it is also a very risky one. It is also very dangerous and can get out of hand if not handled carefully. Traders and investors must understand exactly how to trade options and lots of other details. Getting sufficient knowledge and enough practice is crucial if you are to be successful and consistently profitable.

An option contract can be more expensive at a certain time of the year compared to another period. This is often due to a feature known as time decay. The less time an option has to expiry the less value it has.

An options contract with a distant expiry date is more valuable and will be charged a much higher premium compared to contracts that expire much sooner. As such, all options contracts have a time factor where time is always running. With each passing minute, an options contract loses some of its value. This is a process known as time decay. Within a short period, the value of an options contract will be worthless due to time decay.

VOLATILITY

Another factor that has a huge effect on options is volatility. Volatility tends to raise the option's price. What happens is that there is uncertainty because that is what volatility does. Large price swings are likely to appear should the price of the underlying security increase.

Large price swings tend to increase the probability of something happening. If there are substantial movements in the underlying security, then it means that if the movements are large enough, it would affect the price. As such, volatility is one of the largest and most important aspects of trading options.

TRIGGERS

One of the first things that you need to do after placing a trader is to dial down for triggers. This is one way of managing risks and lowering your risks. When you lower down your risks, you improve your chances of success and as such, you can go for great size.

To achieve this successfully, you will need a chart that makes use of Fibonacci symmetry and retracement. Such a chart will have a slanted line and an upper line. Find the upper line because it is the trigger line. This line indicates or points to the nearest level that has to be broken just so you may continue with the upward trend.

As a trader, you should endeavor to identify a pathway to enter the trade at a point that is nearer to the market's determined turning point. To find such an entry point, you will do what is known as down dialing.

BUYING AND SELLING CALL AND PULL OPTIONS

As it is, there are four distinct things that traders can do with options. They can buy call options, sell options, buy put options, and sell put options. When a trader buys securities, they generally assume a long position. However, buying options only introduces potential which means traders assume potential long positions with options.

Similarly, selling short security introduces a short position. In the same way, selling an uncovered or naked call option introduces a potential short position. These are the four main situations that the options traders can expect to encounter.

Call and put holders are also known as buyers. They have a right but no obligation to sell or buy their options contracts. They can choose to exercise their inherent rights or decide not to do so. This will depend on several factors such as the reasons for trading options and so on. It also introduces a limit to risk exposure so that only the premium can be lost.

Those who write calls and put options contracts on the other hand must sell the underlying security should the buyers choose to exercise their rights. This is bound to happen should an option expire in-the-money. The seller will be expected to fulfill an obligation entered into with the buyer.

This also helps to minimize the risk to the buyer while exposing sellers to almost unlimited risks. Options writers are prone to losing a lot more than the profit they receive from premiums.

There are various reasons why traders and investors use options. Here is a look at some of these reasons. Understanding them is crucial as it demonstrates the practical application of trading options.

FOR SPECULATIVE PURPOSES

Some use options for speculative purposes. Speculation can be termed as a bet or wager regarding price direction shortly. Speculators think that the price of a security, and in some cases assets, will go up or down in the coming months. They arrive at this conclusion based on technical or fundamental analysis.

Based on their predictions, a speculator will then choose to purchase the stock or better still buy call option based on the said stock. A lot of traders prefer speculating via options as they get to enjoy some leverage. A trader could end up spending much less if they opt for options rather than buying stock directly.

OPTIONS FOR HEDGING PURPOSES

The main purpose of trading options is hedging. Hedging is a technique used by traders and all other individuals, organizations, and especially business owners to protect their investments against future shocks. For instance, an airline may hedge on the price of oil for purposes of obtaining favorable oil prices should prices rise in the future.

This is why experts also view hedging as a form of insurance cover. People insure their cars against hazards, homes against disasters, and so on. Hedging provides another way of protecting an investment while minimizing and even limiting potential losses. This is where options come in handy. Options provide traders, and any other person for that matter, with an opportunity to limit risks on the downside while benefiting from the upside through a cost-effective manner.

HOW TO BUY CALL OPTIONS

When you buy a call option, you are also making a long call trade. This is a pretty simple and straightforward process. What you have to focus on is to take advantage of an upward trend in the market. Buying an option is considered the most basic and also the most popular way of investing in options. You will have several options once you purchase call options. These include:

- Selling the options,
- Purchasing the underlying stocks, and
- Allowing the option to expire.

Remember that when you invest in a call option, you receive the right to purchase the underlying stock. However, you are not obligated to do so. The reason why you invest in a call option is simply that you think that the price of the underlying stock will rise. You will want to sell the option at a higher price than what you paid for to cash in and make a profit.

BUYING PUT OPTIONS

Apart from buying a call option, you can choose to buy a put option. This strategy allows investors and traders to earn profits on the downward trend. Put options generally provide opportunities to profit on the downside. Apart from profiting, buying put options allows you to hedge your stock if you expect them to lose value in the coming months.

When you invest your money in a put option, you earn the right to sell a stock at an indicated price. However, selling the stock is never any obligation on your part. If you are an investor, you would buy put options if you believe a stock is headed down in the coming days or weeks. In this instance, you will be exposed to a lower risk instead of shorting on the stock. This strategy can also offer you excellent liquidity as well as leverage.

Chapter 5

START TRADING OPTIONS PROFITABLY IN THE MARKET – HERE'S HOW

In trading, there is a high percentage of suffering losses and which finally concludes to loss of capital. Every trader suffers this in its initial trading condition. But he or she should not back out and learn a lesson from their losses. One cannot simply become a good trader. He or she needs to learn the functioning of the option and should have a proper plan and execute them well.

If a trader is not into a live trade, he or she will never be able to find out his or her comfort zone and time check. It's analyzed and seen many good traders will have completely no idea about the stock market up down for a single day, but they feel they will be right about the same stock market condition in a long-time span. Some day traders will give an idea about a short period in the stock market but will be simply blank about the stock market condition in the long run.

SETTING UP A REASONABLE EXPECTATION

A trader who is starting up should always have the patience to wait to know a market and should not expect that he or she would profit from their trading options. A new trader should never have high expectations when they are just into the market. Rather they should be mentally prepared for losing capital rather than gaining capital. A trader should always begin to expect at least a minimum market experience of a year or a half. This can be illustrated very simply in any field. A famous successful person always bears time and patience to be the greatest achiever in their field.

STARTING WITH A TRADE

A simple question may arise in every new trader's mind on how to begin or start a trade. The answer is even simpler to this question if he or she has decided they should get started with it. He or she can simply startup with a small brokerage firm and startup with a small trading option.

A trader must remember a few things in his or her mind by starting up with small trades like:

- They should have properly planned execution.
- They should not mix up emotions and professions, they should have good control over it.
- They should be able to plan and execute well as they do not have much of the risk factor involved.

Most importantly they should learn to manage capital. There is a large advantage of starting with small trade as one would get to know whether his or her idea is profitable or not.

PROOF CONCEPT

If a trader starts with small trade, he or she will not only gain experience but will also save time. Noises of the stock market do not affect the small traders but if a trader starts with big trading options, he or she will react to these noises in the stock market. A new trader will be in a bad situation with such reactions and the early period. Starting with a small trade will teach a trader to manage capital which is very much necessary. A trader remembers all trades are not the same. A good trader will generate great ideas after the proper experience. A trader must always have records and check on them to see what idea works for them and what does not.

PROPER SORTING AND RECORD-KEEPING

A good successful trader should always keep a record of a few important things of the market like:

- The trader should keep a record of orders placed and quantity involved in it and money made out of it.

- The trader should keep in mind implied volatility and its reference to the current condition.

- The trader should keep in mind about his competitors in the market in that particular trade.

- When the traders begin to keep a record and maintain records they begin to move towards success and chances of being in an odd position are also reduced.

GOOD POSITION OF THE TRADER

Once a trader has achieved his or her position in a trade or stock market, there are frequent ups and downs. A good position trader must know how to react to these situations. By small trade, he or she won't be much affected by the noise of the stock market.

The trader should keep in mind about buying the stock exchange at the perfect time. When a trader does so he or she can perfectly be in the market and understand well.

PROPER EVALUATION OF THE POSITION

A trader must decide very well that a few decisions like backing out on losses must be decided well according to the perfect time.

There are few other decisions like a plan suddenly executed and whether he or she should move on with the profit or go for more?

Even if the sudden plan does not work out then he or she must have a backup and move on forward ahead and not repent on his or her loss and look for a new fresh start.

ABSENCE OF GUARANTEES IN TRADE

It is true there are no guarantees in trading. Even experienced traders fail at times, it is quite natural. The traders should always remember there are very fewer chances of guarantees in trading. Most educators tend to be in a bad reputation, but it does not mean giving up. This can be illustrated very simply, there are coaches for a sportsman to upgrade and succeed over there bad times. They simply do not back out and the same goes for trading and traders.

HARD WORK IS THE ONLY WAY TO SUCCESS

It's easy to advise and listen to it. But when it comes up to the execution of the advice it's not that easy as things do not turn up the way it's told.

The simple way is to start with a small trade and have a lot of patience. A trader should make proper planning for execution. The trader should learn about the market and get into a good position and stick well to it and work very hard to achieve success and be a good disciplined successful trader.

YOUR BROKER

Question: Who is the only person in the market that always makes money? It's your broker! The middleman who takes a small cut of every trade you make does have to fulfill several capital and regulatory requirements but the adage that the best business in the stock market is to be a broker is very true.

This doesn't mean to say that you ought to consider your broker your enemy. Far from it. It's just that you must understand your broker's primary duty is to execute your order. It is not to recommend or advise you on how to trade or what to buy or sell. So don't be picking up the phone asking for advice from such an entity, no matter what the marketing says.

Brokers will require you to satisfy several requirements before being able to trade. Let's look at these now.

Brokers can be roughly divided into two types, and no I don't mean as weasels and even bigger weasels. I'm referring to full service and discount brokers. A full-service broker usually has financial advisors on board who can help you out with your retirement account and such. These brokers usually have phone service which you can call to place your trades and such.

A discount broker adopts a more bare-bones approach. Aside from a trading terminal, you're unlikely to receive anything else. While discount brokers these days have sophisticated trading interfaces, a full-service broker will always be a better bet if your account size is large.

OPTION TRADING FOR BEGINNERS

Chapter 6

CREATING YOUR TRADING SYSTEM

WHAT IS AN OPTIONS TRADING SYSTEM?

There are hundreds of sites, financier firms, and trading administrations that need to sell you their system. Not very many can portray what an options trading system is.

At its center, an options trading system is a strategy for producing buy and sell signals through a tried technique for stock examination. The system can be founded on an options strategy and incorporates both principal and specialized investigation. Options trading systems may center around changes in underlying stock price, unpredictability, time rot, strange buy/sell action, or a blend of these components.

HOW IMPORTANT IS AN OPTIONS TRADING SYSTEM?

The options market is exceptionally perplexing. Trading options without a system resemble building a house without an outline. Instability, time, and stock development would all be able to influence your gainfulness. You should be conscious of every one of these factors. It is anything but trying to be swayed by feeling when the market is moving. Having a system controls your response to those extremely personal and ordinary feelings. How regularly have you sat and watched a trade lose cash the moment your buy arranges filled?

Or on the other hand, have you at any point watched a stock skyrocket in price while you are contemplating whether or not to buy it? Having an organized arrangement set up is urgent to settle on sound and target trading choices. By making and following a good system, you can sharpen your trading executions to be as deadpan and programmed as a PC.

POINTS OF INTEREST OF AN OPTIONS TRADING SYSTEM

OBJECTIVITY

A good option trading system depends on quantifiable criteria that trigger buy and sell signals. It takes the subjectivity and second speculating out of your trading so you can center around preset variables that make for an unstable trade.

ADAPTABILITY

Nearly all options traders will disclose to you that options consider flexibility in your trading. Openings in the options market make it amazingly simple to benefit from here and now positions. With profit occasions and week after week options, you can fabricate procedures for medium-term gains with naturally defined hazard. There are a few ways to benefit in any market condition from slanting to go bound.

SECURITY

An options trading system dependent on a suitable strategy for winning market conditions can go about as support against different speculations. Protective puts are generally utilized along these lines.

HAZARD

A good options trading system limits chance in two vital ways. The principal road is cost. The price of options is low contrasted with buying a similar measure of stock. The second way is identified with stops. A good system will cut misfortunes rapidly and keep them little.

ANY OPTION TRADER CAN DEVELOP AN OPTIONS TRADING SYSTEM

As a trader, it is vital to form a system that uses diverse kinds of option procedures: press condors, broken wing butterflies, schedule spreads, back proportions, straddles, chokes, and collars. It may seem like an outside dialect at present, however, chip away at the vocabulary one exercise at a time. Separate it piece by piece and make it your own. Each term has a particular application for returning benefits under certain market conditions. Learn them all at your own pace to upgrade upon and construct your options trading system.

The more devices that are in your toolkit, the more set you up will be for changing market conditions. If the market were to carry on similarly consistently, trading would be easy breezy. With the end goal to begin in building up your options trading system, you need to make a trading plan or outline to manage you the correct way. Start with an essential system and change it to define your trading criteria and sharpen your system. It requires investment and experience to manufacture an effective options trading system that can return one hundred percent or more in reliably productive trades. When you are happy with the parameters of your order, you can investigate having your very own product made for mechanized trading.

STEPS TO GET STARTED WITH AN OPTIONS TRADING SYSTEM

PICK A STRATEGY

You can pick any plan to begin constructing a system. Buying calls and puts are the most straightforward way to start. As you learn and encounter more about how prices move, you can add new procedures to your trading to upgrade your system. Including secured calls and protective puts to the long value, positions are a legitimate subsequent stage and can supercharge your record by creating month to month or week after week income.

TRADE

Once you have defined the fundamentals of your strategy, the time has come to trade. Begin little, a couple of agreements, and keep point by point records of your exchanges. Make sure to incorporate what the underlying stock price was at the time of your option buy or deal. Your files will enable you to break down how you are getting along and where you can move forward. When you add new trading criteria to your system, you ought to have the capacity to see an enhancement to your measurements. On the off chance that you don't, the time has come to reassess your defined criteria.

ASSESS

Evaluate your victories and disappointments. The recurrence of your examination will rely upon the amount you are trading. If you are trading effectively, a week by week or month to month survey is imperative. Contrast your misfortunes and your rewards. Focus on the key factors that make up a successful trade and endeavor to fine-tune your criteria to improve your executions. As disturbing as it might be, dissect your oversights, as well. Fine-tune your criteria to dispose of committing those similar errors once more. Investigating your missteps is similarly as, if not increasing, critical as concentrating your fruitful trades.

MODIFY

When you have a losing streak or detect a potential powerless territory in your options trading system, alter it. There is no disgrace in being off-base. That is a piece of the matter of trading. The scandal is in being oblivious to your oversights and rehashing them. By sustaining your self-image and defending your shortcoming with reasons, you are ensured to flop in trading. By recognizing your vulnerable sides and making modifications, you can keep your system by changing market patterns and conditions. It sounds so straightforward, yet it requires diligence and order.

LEARN

A trading system isn't static. Keep your mind dynamic by always learning. The more you examine the stock market and options trading system, the more you will know, and the happier you will be. On the off chance that an options trading system resembled a tic-tac-toe system, we would all be well off. Fortunately, options trading isn't as exhausting as a tyke's amusement. Gain some new useful knowledge consistently and ingest it into your options trading system.

Chapter 7
GETTING STARTED

You may be excited to jump into the market and start trading right away, but there are a few things that you will need to do first. You will need to start with a good understanding of the basics that come with options and you need to know some of the option types that you can pick from. We talked about these topics a little bit before, but the more that you can learn about them before investing, the more success you will have.

After you have had some time to understand what options all are about and what you will be getting yourself into, it is time to come up with your motivation for trading. Ask yourself how much money you are looking to make from this trade and how you would like to use that money when you have earned it. This motivation will help you out so much when you are in the thick of the trading and you need some help staying focused.

But one of the most important things that you will need to focus on when you first get started is having what is called a trading plan. The trading plan will list all of the things that you want to be able to accomplish while you are trading. It can include what you expect to happen, some of your goals, the strategy that you will go with, and any other guidelines that will help you be successful. Those who decide to start investing in options without having a good plan in place will be the ones who run into a lot of risks.

GETTING A BROKER

The second thing that you will want to do is find the broker you would like to work with. The broker is the person who works with you and often will be able to give you advice and help you to make the trades that you want. All brokers that you go with will require some fees or a commission that you will need to pay to use their services, so you must factor this in when figuring out the costs that you want to incur. There are many different types of brokers that you can go with and the price that you pay will depend on the type and amount of services you choose to go with.

When you pick out the broker you want to work with, you will probably need to meet with them in the beginning and discuss your trading plan and how they will be able to help. They will go over a risk assessment with you so they know where you stand with the number of risks that you are willing to take. It is a good place for you and the broker to get started together so you are on the same page and can get things done.

CHOOSING THE ASSETS

When you are working with an option, you are working with a contract that covers the asset, rather than the asset itself. There are quite a few underlying assets that you can go with when picking out options. You will be able to sell and purchase these contracts and the assets can include things like commodities, foreign currencies, bonds, stocks, and more. This is good news to the investors because it will give you a lot of options and you will be able to pick out the asset that you are most comfortable with using. Of course, you need to stop and do some research ahead of time so that you pick out a good asset that will make you money.

HOW TO MANAGE YOUR RISK AND MONEY

As a beginner of investing in options, you must earn the best ways to manage your money and risks. Like with the other investments that you can make, options can be risky and those who decide to jump into the market without a good plan in place will end up losing a ton of money in the process. When you are working on your trading plan, you should make sure to include guidelines on the risks that you are willing to take and how much money you will use.

This is why it is so important for you to get that trading plan in place right from the beginning and then keep it in place. Having this plan decided will help you to keep your emotions out of the game. As soon as the emotions start to come into play, it is time to leave the market because these emotions are just going to lead you to make horrible trading decisions. Before you decide to make any decisions in trading, it is a good idea to take some deep breaths, take a look over the plan, and then decide how you will behave.

One thing that you can keep in mind when you are trying to manage your money and your risks are the option spread. The option spread will combine more than one position on the contract using the same security. This way, regardless of how the market ends up going, you can make some money rather than losing it all.

DIVERSIFYING YOUR PORTFOLIO

You should also consider how you will arrange your portfolio. The more different types of investments that you can add to the portfolio, the easier it is to limit your risks and get the best results. You may want to consider working with a variety of investment choices such as options, currencies, stocks, and more. There are even many choices for diversifying just by working with options.

POSITION SIZING

This may sound like it will add in a lot of work, but the process is simple and will help you out. All that position sizing means is that you must decide how much money, or how much of the capital that you plan to use on one specific position while you are trading. It is similar to what you will do with diversifying because you will spread out your money rather than using it all in one position. It also allows you to be more in control of your capital, you will have more control over your losses and can prevent yourself from losing a lot of money in the process.

PLANNING YOUR TRADES

After you have had some time to finish out the other steps above, it is now time to sit down with your broker and decide what you need to do to start with options trading. Some of the steps that we will do during this part will include:

Forecasting: With this part, you will make some predictions about what will happen in the future with your security, such as whether or not it will fall or rise soon. This forecast will help you to determine the best strategy that you can use and can even help you to decide which option will work with your chosen strategy.

SETTING GOALS

Here, you need to come up with some goals that you should follow during your trades. Ask yourself a few questions before you get started, such as: how much you would like to make from the trade? This will make it easier to determine if you were successful with the trade when it is all over.

CHOOSE YOUR STRATEGY

There are a ton of strategies that you can work with when you choose options trading and we will take some time to discuss them more later. But it is so important to pick out a good strategy and keep it in place if you would like to be successful. Before you tell your broker what you want to get done with a trade, you must pick out a good strategy to help you out.

CHOOSE THE POSITION SIZING

In this step, you will just decide on how much money you will invest in each option. This helps you to determine which risks you will face before you even get started.

MAKING YOUR TRADES

Once you have sat down with your broker and determined the steps above, it is time for you both to decide which trades you want to work with. The broker will be able to help you to set up your funds so that you can get some of these orders done fast. When you are entering into a new trade you want to make sure that you have the funds in place so that you are not missing out because it took too long to get the money. Showing your broker your plan, or at least writing out the plan so you know it ahead of time, can help you to stay on track.

MONITORING THE TRADES

After you have worked with your broker to place your orders and all of the trades are done, there are still some things that you will need to get done. It is never a good idea to just put in your money to the option and then just ignore it in the hopes that you will make money. Instead, you must learn how to spend your time monitoring the trades to see how they are doing.

What this means is that you must watch the trade, rather than just ignoring it. You have to keep records of what is going on throughout time with your chosen option so that you can make smart decisions about when to use the option, when to hold onto it, or when you may want to give up and cut your losses. The choices that you make during this stage will depend on whether you are making a profit or a loss on your option. And how are you supposed to know whether you are doing well or not if you never pay attention to the option?

And those are the simple steps that you need to keep in mind when you are ready to get started with options trading and making money. If you can come up with a good strategy to help you trade, you can pick out a good option and get on it at a good time, and you do not let the emotions get into the mix, then you will be able to make a good amount of money on your investment. It is tough to do these investments sometimes, but they can be worth it when you start making some money.

Chapter 8
THE ROLE PLAYED BY OPTIONS EXCHANGES

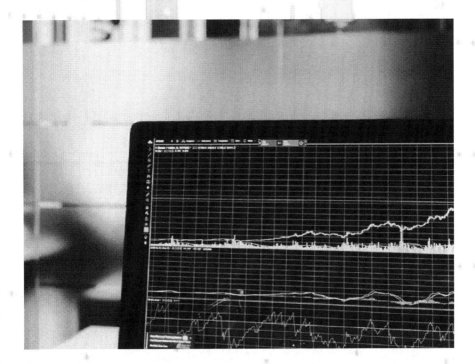

The options exchanges play a critical role in ensuring that there are enough securities to base options contracts on. The following are some of the significant functions of an options exchange.

LIQUIDITY

Perhaps the biggest function of options exchanges is to ensure ready markets for options contracts. The markets ensure that holders of options can exercise their options and that there are enough buyers to purchase the options. Traders are looking for avenues to increase their earning potential, and liquidity helps them achieve that. Options contracts have a time limit unlike other securities such as shares, which necessitates liquidity. The existence of market makers is particularly responsible for liquidity.

GAUGING A COUNTRY'S ECONOMY

The state of an options market can reliably inform us what the country's economic situation is like. The most common underlying assets that traders base their options on are shares. The prevailing economic conditions are always reflected in the share prices of various companies. If the country is experiencing prosperity, the share prices will be up, and if the country is experiencing market crashes, the share prices will go down. Thus, the options exchanges play a critical role in ensuring that traders have a sense of how their country is performing economy-wise. Stocks are the pulse of an economy, and they are accurate predictors of a country's economic state.

SECURITIES PRICING

Options traders have a wide pool to choose from when it comes to underlying assets. However, the value of an underlying asset is determined by the options exchange according to the forces of demand and supply. The financial securities of prosperous companies are worth more than the securities of moderately successful companies. The valuation of securities is important not only for traders but also for governments. Governments levy taxes on earnings drawn from options trading, so they first have to get the value of the securities.

SAFETY OF TRANSACTIONS

Traders want to be sure that they can trust all the parties that they are getting into business with. Therefore, it is the work of an options exchange to ensure the players are trustworthy. For one, most options contracts are based on financial securities of publicly listed companies, and these companies must operate within stringent rules and regulations. Thus, the trader is assured of security when dealing with other parties. The options markets should provide all relevant information about options contracts and securities to discourage the trader from making a move out of ignorance.

PROVIDING SPECULATION SCOPE

Speculation of securities is critical to ensure a healthy balance of demand and supply of securities. Many traders earn their profits from purely speculative risk. They have developed a skill of determining the movement of prices. The options exchanges provide traders with the resources and tools of speculating on the securities performance, thus allowing traders to earn profits.

PROMOTES INVESTMENT CULTURE

Options exchanges are critical in promoting the culture of investing in valuable securities like the stock as opposed to unproductive assets such as precious metals. Traders have a wide selection of underlying securities to base their options contracts on; thus, they are not limited in the range of their strategies. A strong saving and investment culture is critical for the economic advancement of a country.

THE CONTINUOUS MARKET FOR SECURITIES

Options exchanges allow traders to base their options on a wide range of underlying securities, and in case of any risks, traders are at liberty to switch from one security to the next. This is different from purchasing stocks wherein you are stuck with the consequences of poor decisions.

CAPITAL FORMATION

Options exchanges promote the pooling together and redistribution of resources. The exchanges create a win-win situation for both sides. Companies raise capital when their stocks are publicly listed, and their securities act as the underlying. On the other hand, traders stand to benefit from the high earning potential and low-capital requirements for options contracts. So, options exchanges play a critical role in ensuring that the parties are in a position to generate capital.

CONTROL COMPANIES

The significance of transparency within the derivatives market cannot be overstated. If a trader has the misfortune of working with shady companies, they could easily lose their earnings. Options exchanges make it hard for shady companies to spoil the market. For instance, publicly-traded companies have to submit relevant documents and adhere to certain performance standards as doing so will boost investor confidence. Companies that refuse to cooperate with exchanges are blacklisted from the market.

FISCAL AND MONETARY POLICIES

The fiscal policy and the monetary policy of the government must not hurt the players in the financial industry. Options exchanges facilitate the creation and execution of key policies that will govern the financial markets.

PROPER CANALIZATION OF WEALTH

Options are a great way of putting capital into great use, as opposed to having the capital just sitting around. Thus, the economy benefits from an injection of capital which would otherwise have been inactive. The injection of capital into the economy promotes wealth distribution and fights off economic disgraces like unemployment.

EDUCATION PURPOSES

Options trading features complex processes. Even people who claim to understand options trading might be low-key deluded. Thus, the importance of education cannot be overstated. Many traders just get the hang of things and set about purchasing and selling options contracts, forgetting that it is critical to first educate one's self. Options exchanges provide a wealth of resources and information that are meant to enlighten traders. Empowered traders improve trading activity.

Chapter 9
THE OPTIONS TRADER MINDSET AND PSYCHOLOGY

When it comes to making money trading options, you must remember that you must control your emotions at all times, something that is easier said than done, especially if you are in the moment and have just taken an unexpected loss. Cultivating the proper mindset can be done with practice, however, and doing so will make it easier for you to face the early parts of your options trading career with the proper expectations regarding what sort of results you can expect from options trading. Specifically, this means that you will need to understand that investing in options isn't a quick and easy path to success and, rather, is sure to take plenty of dedication and hard work if you hope to reap the potential rewards.

The first step to finding success via options trading is to get your emotions in check. The best traders are robotic, they only rely on the facts and they follow their trading plan 100 percent of the time. If you find yourself getting extremely emotional as far as trading is concerned then you must start by keeping a log of the emotions you have while trading, and the results of those emotions on your trading outcome. While this might seem unnecessary at first, you will be surprised how helpful having a clear outline of your patterns is when it comes to improving your overall trade percentage in the long term.

The fact of the matter is that if you ever hope to successfully trade options then you will need to know you can stick with your plan no matter what the emotional part of your mind is telling you to do. A good plan is one that remains successful, not 100 percent of the time, or even 95 percent of the time and instead manages to be successful roughly 60 percent of the time. While 60 percent is certainly enough to ensure you turn a profit, it is not enough that it allows for additional wiggle room in the terms of letting your emotions talk you into going off the book at every turn. Remember, trading options is a numbers game, and keeping your emotions in check is key to not working with skewed data.

A lot of traders are largely focused on trading and earning profits. They are hardly ever concerned about the mindset and how they are supposed to handle emotions and feelings as they trade. A lot of the time they focus on trades and celebrate when they win while feeling bad when they lose. This is not the best approach according to experts.

To be a successful trader, it is crucial to understand the reasons why some trades do not work out and why some lose money. By understanding why some trades lose money, it becomes possible to make adjustments so that these can be minimized as much as possible.

All traders, even the most experienced win some trades and lose some. The difference is the number of losses and reasons for the losses. Skilled traders can discern with relative accuracy the directions of the markets and chances of making winning trades. However, it is really difficult for anyone to perform better than the markets.

No trader can outperform the market, yet most traders are unable to grasp this simple principle. The most crucial initial step is to select winning trades. This is a skill that needs to be learned. A trader should have an edge as this increases the chances of winning. If a trader has no edge, then he or she can only emerge victorious about half the time.

There are two things that an options trader should focus on. The first is to ensure to earn a profit of at least 50% or more. Also, money lost from any losing trades should not exceed that earned from winning trades. This calls for some skill development. An options trader should take time to develop the necessary skills on how to identify such trades.

YOU CAN WEATHER THE STORM

Options prices can move a lot throughout short periods. So, someone who likes to see their money protected and not losing any is not going to be suitable for options trading. Now, we all want to come out ahead, so I am not saying that you have to be happy about losing money to be an options trader. What you have to be willing to do is calmly observe your options losing money, and then be ready to stick it out to see gains return in the future. This is akin to riding a real roller coaster, but it is a financial roller coaster. Options do not slowly appreciate the way a Warren Buffett investor would hope to see. Options move big on a percentage basis, and they move fast. If you are trading multiple contracts at once, you might see yourself losing $500 and then earning $500 over a matter of a few hours. In this sense, although most options traders are not "day traders" technically speaking, you will be better off if you have a little bit of a day trading mindset.

YOU DON'T MAKE EMOTIONAL DECISIONS

Since options are, by their nature, volatile, and very volatile for many stocks, coming to options trading and being emotional about it is not a good way to approach your trading. If you are emotional, you will exit your trades at the wrong time in 75% of cases. You don't want to make any sudden moves when it comes to trading options. As we have said, you should have a trading plan with rules on exiting your positions, stick to those rules and you should be fine.

BE A LITTLE BIT MATH-ORIENTED

To understand options trading and be successful, you cannot be shy about numbers. Options trading is a numbers game. That doesn't mean you have to drive over to the nearest university and get a statistics degree. But if you do understand probability and statistics, you are a better options trader. Frankly, it's hard to see how you can be a good options trader without having a mind for numbers. Some math is at the core of options trading and you cannot get around it.

YOU ARE MARKET-FOCUSED

You don't have to set up a day trading office with ten computer screens so you can be tracking everything by the moment, but if you are hoping to set up a trade and lazily come back to check it three days later, that isn't going to work with options trading. You do need to be checking your trades a few times a day. You also need to be keeping up with the latest financial and economic news, and you need to keep up with any news directly related to the companies you invest in or any news that could impact those companies. If the news does come out, you will need to make decisions if it's news that isn't going to be favorable to your positions. Also, you need to be checking the charts periodically, so you have an idea of where things are heading for now.

OPTIONS TRADERS ARE FLEXIBLE

Most frequently, people do what they have been brainwashed to do and they will trade call options hoping to profit from rising share prices. If you are in that mindset now, you need to challenge yourself and begin trading in different ways, so you can experience making money from declining stock prices, or in the case of iron condors, stock prices that don't even change at all. You need to be able to adapt to changing market conditions to profit as an options trader. So, don't entrap yourself by only using one method.

TAKE A DISCIPLINED APPROACH

Don't just buy options for a certain stock because it feels good. You need to research your stocks. That will include doing fundamental analysis. This will mean paying attention to the history of a stock, knowing what the typical ranges are for, stock in recent history is, and also reading through the company's financial statements and prospectus. Remember, I suggest picking three companies to trade options on for a year and also two index funds. The index funds require less research, but for the three companies that you pick, you should get to know those companies inside and out. Stick with them for a year, at the end of each year, evaluate each company. Then decide if you want to keep them and bring them forward into the following year's trades. If one company is not working out for you, then move on and try a different company.

CONTROLLING YOUR EMOTIONS (TRADING PSYCHOLOGY)

Trading psychology is the mental state and emotions that determine the success or failure of trading options. It represents the aspect of your behavior that dictates the decisions you make when faced with a trade. Psychology is vital to any trade and can be compared to experience, knowledge, and skills in determining your success as a trader.

When you decide to start options trading, you need to grasp the concept of risk-taking and discipline that determines the implementation of any trade.

The two most common emotions are greed and fear, while others are regret and hope.

FEAR

At any given time, fear represents one of the worst kinds of emotions that you can have. Check-in your newspaper one day, and you read about a steep selloff, and the next thing is trying to rack your brain about what to do next even if it isn't the right action at that time.

Many investors think that they know what will happen in the next few days, which makes them have a lot of confidence in the outcome of the trade. This leads to investors getting into the trade at a level that is too high or too low, which in turn makes them react emotionally.

As the trader puts a lot of hope on the single trade, the level of fear tends to increase, and hesitation and caution kick in.

Fear is part of every trader, but skilled traders can manage fear. There are various types of fears that you will experience, let us look at a few of them:

Have you ever entered a trade and all you could think about is losing? The fear of losing makes it hard for you to execute the perfect strategy or enter or exit a strategy at the right time.

As a trader, you know that you need to make timely decisions when the strategy signals you to take one. When you have fear guiding you, the level of confidence drops, and you can't execute the strategy the right way, at the right time. When a strategy fails, you lose trust in your abilities as well as strategy.

When you lose trust in many of the strategies, you end up with analysis paralysis, whereby you can't pull the trigger on any decision that you make. Making a move becomes a huge challenge.

When you cannot pull the trigger, all you can think about is staying away from the pain of losing, while you need to move towards gains.

No trader likes to lose, but it is a fact that even the best traders will make losses once in a while. The key is for them to make more profitable trades that allow them to stay in the game.

When you worry too much, you end up being distracted from your execution process, and instead, you focus on the results.

To reduce the fear of trading, you need to accept losses. The probability of losing or making a profit is 50/50, and you need to accept this fact and accept a trade, whether it is a sell or a buy signal.

GREED

This refers to a selfish desire to get more money than you need from a trade. When the desire to get more than you can usually make takes over your decision-making process, you are looking at failure.

Greed is seen to be more detrimental than fear. Yes, fear can make you lose trades, but the good thing is that you get to preserve your capital. On the other hand, greed places you in a situation where you spend your capital faster than you return it. It pushes you to act when you shouldn't be acting at all.

When you are greedy, you end up acting irrationally. Irrational trading behavior can be overtrading, overleveraging, holding onto trades for too long, or chasing different markets.

The more greed you have, the more foolish you act. If you reach a point at which greed takes over from common sense, then you are overdoing it.

When you are greedy, you also end up risking way much more than you can handle, and you end up with a loss. You also have unrealistic expectations from the market, which makes it seem as if you are after just money and nothing else.

When you are greedy, you also start trading prematurely without any knowledge of the options trading market.

When you are too greedy, your judgment is clouded, and you won't think about any negative consequences that might result when you make certain decisions.

Many traders that were too greedy ended up giving up after making this mistake in the initial trading phase.

Like any other endeavor in trading, you need a lot of effort to overcome greed. It might not be easy because we are talking about human emotions here, but it is possible.

First, you have to know that every call you make won't be the right one at all times. There are times when you won't make the right move, and you will end up losing money. At times you will miss the perfect strategy altogether, and you won't move a step ahead.

Secondly, you have to agree that the market is way bigger than you. When you do this, you will accept and make mistakes in the process.

HOPE

Hope is what keeps a trading expectation alive when it has reached reversal. Hope is usually factored in the mind of a trader that has placed a huge amount on a trade. Many traders also go for hope when they wish to recoup past losses. These traders are always hopeful that the next trade will be the best, and they end up placing more than they should on the trade.

This type of emotion is dangerous because the market doesn't care at all about your hopes and will take your money.

REGRET

This is the feeling of disappointment or sadness over a trade that has been done, especially when it has resulted in a loss.

Focusing too much on missing trade makes the trader not to move forward. After you learn the lessons after such a loss, you need to understand the mistakes you made then move ahead.

When you decide to let regret rule your thinking, you start chasing markets with the hopes that you will end up making money on a position by doubling the entrance price.

THINGS THAT DISTINGUISH WINNING AND LOSING TRADERS IN OPTIONS TRADING

HANDLING ANALYSIS PARALYSIS

Traders usually start their journey getting the right knowledge. This knowledge comes in the form of books, coaches, and more. Once you have the information, the next step is to take it and use it in the market. The lucky ones will place various trades, and then things will go their way, while for others, the money will go down the drain.

Trading requires you to determine the right time to place a trade or exit one. The successful trader will know when to use a strategy, but the losing trader will end up placing trade after trade without any success at all.

UNDERSTANDING THE NATURE OF THE MARKET

You need to understand that no market is constant – it changes with time. At times, the market will go along with your analysis, while at times; it might go the opposite direction.

ACCEPT THE RISK

No one wants to lose money on the markets. You need to come up with a strategy that allows you to know when to stop and reflect or tap out. At times you have to pull the plug regardless of how much you have invested in research and your expectations.

KNOW WHEN TO TAKE PROFITS

So, what determines the exit strategy? You need to know what point requires you to say this profit is enough for me. At times, it might be dictated by the changes in the trend or your rules of trading. Don't hold on to a trade for too long because it is always better to have some profit than wait and end up losing everything.

UNDERSTANDING WHEN YOU ARE WRONG

You need to remember that the options trading market is random, and you need to admit when you are wrong at times. This is because failure to admit will lead you to greed that might cloud your judgment.

When it comes to trading options, you have various traps that lead to fear or greed. Most of these traps come on expiration day; let us look at the various traps to avoid.

TRAPS TO AVOID ON EXPIRATION DAY

So, it is the day when the options are expiring, and this is the time you have to decide what action to take. If you are a seller, then you are anticipating this time because you hope to make some money out of the trade, while if you are a buyer, then you are dreading losses that might arise.

Either way, you need to be privy to some aspects of trading that will help you avoid any surprises.

Here are top traps that you need to know and avoid at this time.

EXERCISING THE LONG OPTION

You need to consider your options at expiration. At times, you can just close the options trade rather than buying the shares. Remember that when you exercise your options, you have to pay additional broker commissions that might not be ideal for you.

OPTIONS - VARY FROM COUNTRY TO COUNTRY

A huge percentage of the traders on the market use American style options to trade. However, other traders desire to trade the European options, and this comes with differences.

For European options, you can only exercise the option at the time of expiration, while American options give you the chance to exercise the option between the time you show interest till expiration.

For both options, you don't have to be stuck with the position till the expiry.

HOLDING POSITIONS TO THE LAST MINUTE

One of the hardest things to do is to let go of a position that you believe in. There are two scenarios under this – first, you have a losing trade that you just don't want to let go. On the other hand, you might have a position that is making you some money, but you think you have the chance to get more money before the options expire.

When it comes to trading, the final few days are the worst times to exit the trade because of the high risk that is associated with it. This means that the value of the option swings in any direction during these final days. Due to this, you can see your profits disappear in a few seconds!

The good thing is that you can decide to let the options go worthless and retain the premium that you collect at expiration.

ROLLING AN OPTION POSITION

Most investors are convinced that a certain security is way better than another one. Many stock traders think that stock trading is much better than the options because they tend to expire.

If you are on a winning streak, don't hold out longer just to see the close; instead take the chance of closing the deal and making some money, however little. Using the rolling technique, you get to lock the profits in a position and then benefit from the profit. You can do this way early in the trading cycle as opposed to going after it when you need to close the trade.

Rolling gives you the ability to make some profits then use the original investment to pay for another option with a longer expiration period.

ADDITIONAL TRADING PSYCHOLOGY TIPS

There are other things that you need to also keep in mind. For instance, you need to develop and stick with good trading habits. As a trader, you need to note that a winner is one who is persistent and consistent. You should develop the habit of closely studying the markets, conducting your analysis, and position sizing.

Position sizing is especially prevalent in a volatile market. As such, you need to take care of your downside risks and ensure that your position size appropriately. You should also envision the end game. Come up with a vision of where you want the trade to head then prepare to make any necessary adjustments.

You also need to accept any possible failures. Sometimes your strategies will not work out and you will lose some trades. This happens to all traders, even experienced ones. If you assume that you must succeed on each attempt, then you will be setting yourself up for failure.

The first and most important aspect is for a trader to identify one or more strategies that they are very familiar with and comfortable with. Such strategies should be adapted and then applied whenever market conditions permit. For instance, iron condor strategies are best suited for markets whose volatility was initially high but steadily declining. Naked put selling and covered call writing are strategies suitable for a moderately bullish market.

Another crucial skill to learn is technical analysis. Some traders solely rely on this technical skill to enter and exit trades. Technical analysts need to develop their chart reading skills. It is never easy and the process is not learned overnight but takes some time. While there are never any guarantees for success, chances for success are significantly higher when such skills are developed and optimized.

For success, a trader needs to focus on investigating all the signals and cutting losses. The key point in this instance is learning which ones are strong and which ones simply breakeven. Also, all traders should never trade just for the sake of trading. This is because trading is done with an aim and purpose. The purpose is to be profitable. If trades are not working out then it is advisable to pause for a while and take a breather. Traders should only enter trades they have prepared well for and have a suitable plan of execution.

Trading options is a process that revolves mostly around three major factors. These are money management, trading strategies, and psychology. You need to keep in mind that the markets can be a very emotional place, so you must remain focused and disciplined. If you do not stay disciplined, then you will lose out and others will very likely take advantage of you.

What you need to do to trade successfully is to have a solid strategy, follow the strategy, and stick to it. If the strategy does not follow the intended plan, then simply quit and come up with another strategy.

If you have a strong mindset, you will be able to understand when to pursue a losing trade and when to quit. If you lack discipline, then one of two emotions will take over. These are greed and fear.

Sometimes traders trade on a whim and keep posting random trades. Rather than take this approach, you really should focus on a successful strategy which you will pursue until you need to exit. You should also have good trading skills and a proper money management plan. With these in place, you will be able to focus better and think in terms of probabilities and risk-reward ratios. This way, you will not leave room for emotional trading.

Chapter 10

OPTIONS TRADING SOFTWARE

Nowadays, with most options being traded on the web, you must have a ground-breaking software system that will enable you to sell at the best dimension conceivable and make more benefits. An excellent trading software package accomplishes more than essentially will allow you to trade efficiently. Options trading software ought to likewise allow you to buy more intelligent and all the more productively. There are a vast number of trading software packages accessible out there however you will search for similar essential features in all packages to enable you to turn into the best and most productive trader conceivable.

One thing to search for in any options trading software is the accreditations of the organization selling the software. Since there are many systems out there, you will most likely need to ensure that you are utilizing a system that has been attempted and tried by a lot of different traders, both expert and individual, and that the organization has an excellent reputation for conveying quality items.

You will likewise need to have a nearby take a gander at the options investigation software that the system gives. This sort of software will enable you to investigate potential trades before you make them and will educate you on each perspective regarding the trade from a specialized angle. This is crucial not exclusively to maintain a strategic distance from obtrusive oversights that you may have disregarded, yet, also, to enable you to settle on various comparable trades when you have to recognize the best one rapidly.

You will likewise require to have the option to evaluate trades, graphically present the trade to enable you to picture what's going on, and will allow you to make propelled figures and recreations on a business. The majority of this is to enable you to settle on informed and canny choices with the data you need, before you trade.

Just as the power and features of the software itself, what is imperative for most traders beginning is that the organization furnishes you with the majority of the support and data that you require. There will be numerous circumstances where you will require help, now and then finally, and you need an organization that furnishes you with this dimension of support.

Additionally, watch out for packages that software organizations may furnish you with, for example, options trading guidance and procedure that you may discover helpful.

BINARY OPTIONS DEMO ACCOUNT

Opening a demo account managing binary alternatives and with a trusted broker is a fantastic technique to gain proficiency with the binary choices advertised. If you are considering risking money to get into the binary alternatives exchanging, first open a without money exchanging account. Demos will show you how to ace your binary options and give a choice to widen or extend the usefulness of your account, begin a more extensive account, and utilize deferred starter choices.

To end up useful and beneficial, gain dominance of internet exchanging. If you are content with the advancement, you make and find that you are positive about exchanging, band together with the organizations you worked with utilizing their free binary choice demo accounts.

TAKE NO CHANCES BEFORE YOU INVEST

Demo accounts give genuine encounters in exchanging. You effectively participate in trading the present market. Finding out about binary choices incorporates encountering the securities exchange, perusing tables, and following patterns. Build up your exchanging procedure without risking actual money. These accounts offer resources for both the learner and the master broker. Preparing offers availability to broker stages where you can lead no-hazard exchanges. Figure out how to utilize investigation instruments, in addition to using stage highlights.

There are two kinds of these accounts. The most regular account is the standard free account that licenses you get to various exchanging stages, instructive materials, and broker highlights. Official reports don't empower reproduced exchanging. You might need to put resources into a demo account that offers similar informative materials of a standard account, yet gives you the decision to partake in reenacted binary choices exchanging.

There are a few brokers that offer demo accounts total with the chance to take part in recreating exchanging. These brokers are likewise viewed as very respectable and maybe speculation houses that you might need to band together with when you open a first trading account.

BROKER INVESTMENT HOUSES

Option Fair gives a demo account that offers exchanging test systems used to encounter genuine exchanging. This test system provides exchange types to be tried and guidance apparatuses and resources. You approach transferring online courses and instructional exercises to improve your expectation to learn and adapt.

Give a shot to Option Bit, a broker furnishing demo accounts with recreated exchange inside a soundstage. There are e-Courses and preparing to the individuals who have never transferred. In the wake of learning on the demo account, Option Bit offers to exchange instructional exercises and a stage indistinguishable to the demo account.

A third alternative is Banc De Binary. Their account contains $50,000 in exchanging assets to be utilized for the mimicked exchange instructional exercise. You should build up a customer account with a store of $250 before you approach the report. This is somewhat not the same as free binary choices ones, yet if you are not kidding about going into binary alternatives exchanging you will have an enormous favorable position over the individuals who use non-subsidized test systems.

Before going into the universe of binary alternatives exchanging, use demo accounts that will bring you into exchanging without going out on a limb. Exploit the learning procedures to pick up a colossal start in exchange.

ALERTS ABOUT BINARY OPTIONS

Binary choices concerning exchanges that are dependent upon whether the essential resource diminishes or increments in esteem and the financial specialist's forecast of these developments. There are many good brokerage houses and choices exchanging substances that are forthright and clear. These actual exchanging stages publicize quick profit for ventures and offer reproduced exchanging stages and enlisted resources before you start contributing our own money. There are, anyway, brokerages that offer and pitch binary alternatives to speculators without enrolling the securities. This isn't inconsistent with government securities laws. Venture experts caution financial specialists against taking an interest in choices from complex organizations that are advanced on YouTube recordings, Internet-based advisements, or email showcasing.

ALERTS TO NOTE

The SEC documented a grievance against a specific outside binary organization after it started to offer market parallels to U.S financial specialists in 2010. This brokerage house persuaded financial specialists that they could make accounts, store money, and buy pairs with stock records as the real resource. This organization focused on clients with meager salaries and personal esteem. One financial specialist trusted the promotion that he/she could pick up a tremendous venture and incentive on a $300 exchange. Shockingly the $300 was the sole measure of money that this contributor had coming consistently, and there were not securities papers submitted. The customer contributed his whole month to month paycheck, played the binary field, and lost his entire $300 in addition to broker liberties. For example, the customer lost their $300 just like the brokerage expenses that were charged.

Be careful about the potential for extortion in this worthwhile territory of exchanging parallels. You will as a general rule lose your whole speculation even though the chance to pick up in an exceptionally brief time is exceptionally alluring. Check the foundation of brokers and exchanging stages before putting your money into pairs offered by "off the divider brokerages." If you are unfit to acquire foundation data about the organization or decide the monetary expert is enrolled with the SEC, be exceptionally wary. Go somewhere else to put your exchanges.

RECORDS OF PENALTIES

You can discover records of punishments that are surveyed to a specific brokerage house by perusing budgetary diaries. One unregistered organization being referred to get money related disciplines, perpetual orders, and other penury evaluations. Peruse announcements distributed by the SEC's Office of Investor Education and Advocacy in addition to the CFTC's Office of Consumer Outreach. These are announcements that examine the potential danger of putting resources into binary alternatives and caution financial specialists that there is no wellbeing net from unregistered government securities and items. Abstain from obtaining unregistered binary options.

Chapter 11
HOW TO PLACE AN ORDER

You have learned different aspects regarding all the factors that go into making a good options trade, it's time to start putting your new knowledge into action. This is a two-part process, the first part of which is coming up with the right plan and the second is executing that plan in the right way.

WORK OUT A PLAN

Before you can begin trading successfully, the first thing you will need to consider is creating your personalized trading plan. This plan will include several facets that are unique to you and proceeding without taking the time to create your plan is a good way to kill your options trading career before it starts.

START BY CONSIDERING YOUR SKILLS

When it comes to ensuring you have the right options trading plan, the first thing you will want to do is to take a look at your overall skill level and familiarity with trading in general, if not options trading specifically. Many new options traders are tempted to overestimate their skills early on, but this will do nothing but hold you back in the long run. Be honest and accurately catalog your strengths and weaknesses. Specifically, you want to have a clear idea of how likely you will ignore your plan in favor of following your emotions. This is always a folly and if you know it is your tendency you will have to plan around it.

THINK ABOUT OTHER CHALLENGES

When it comes to determining what plan or system works for you, it will be important to take into account any other potential challenges that you might need to face to achieve the level of success that you are hoping for. These types of challenges could be anything from a lack of resources or planning to something more complicated and personal. The point is, anything outside of the normal market inconsistencies that prevent options trading from being purely profitable should be accounted for to ensure your success rate remains as high as possible.

CONSIDER THE RIGHT AMOUNT OF RISK FOR YOU

When it comes to deciding how much risk is the right amount for you, the first thing you will want to do is decide how much your total investment budget is. If you have never invested anything before then this investment budget can be seen as your portfolio. Never put more than 5% of your total into any one trade which makes it difficult to lose anything too substantial all at once. What's more, you will want to determine if the trade is worth the effort by ensuring it will pay off at least 300% when compared with the initial investment.

This is what is known as the risk/reward ratio and it can be found when it comes to any options trade by simply taking the amount of estimated profit and dividing it by the amount of the investment. If the result is greater than or equal to 3 the trade will be worth your time if it pays out. Remember, the return will only happen if the trade works in your favor, however, which can be determined by finding your level of tolerance when it comes to investment risk.

Finding your tolerance level when it comes to risk can be accomplished by taking the amount of time you have available to work on investing versus the number of potential returns you are looking for. This means that the less time you are willing to spend on investing in options, the more risk you will have to be willing to accept if you are hoping to make more than a moderate amount of money from doing so.

DO YOUR HOMEWORK

Every day in the hours before the market opens you need to plan on being in front of some type of screen, learning about everything that happened while you were sleeping and deciding how you think it will affect the markets you are interested in the most. This means checking foreign markets, the premarket forecast, and the index futures to name a few, all in the name of deciding what the market's mood of the day is after the day gets going properly and trading begins.

You will also want to always be aware of any upcoming due dates for earning data to be reported which will always disrupt the market in question in one way or another. Companies have to report their earnings in comparison to their projections 4 times a year and the results are almost always going to affect the market seriously. The right choice in these instances is to wait until the rash of panic trading has passed and get in once things begin to stabilize but not so much so that there is no longer a profit to be made by doing so.

DECIDE ON AN EXIT STRATEGY

No matter what plan or strategy you settle on, you must have a clear idea of what an acceptable level of profit or loss means to you and setting a firm exit strategy accordingly. While it can be tempting to wait on an underlying stock to rebound before exercising your option or walking away, the results are rarely going to end in your favor and it can lead to a bad habit of hanging on to sub-par trades that could cost you big in the long term. The right exit strategy for you will vary based on how much risk you can accept, coupled with how many trades you are planning to make each day and what level of micromanaging you are comfortable with. Regardless, the point at which you decide to bail on a bad trade should be the same for all of your trades.

Setting up an effective exit strategy begins by deciding where the appropriate point to set what is known as a stop-loss is. A stop loss is an automated order that you put in when you purchase the option which indicates at what point you want the option to automatically be sold. It is used to minimize your losses if a trade suddenly starts heading in the opposite direction you were hoping it would. You should avoid setting stop losses on options with extremely volatile because they are likely going to fluctuate too much to make them truly effective in this instance.

Stop orders are useful if you are the writer as well as the holder because they can be used to ensure that additional options are purchased if the price rises instead. You will also sometimes find it useful to use a secondary stop order which will sell if the price then hits a secondary amount. This is considered the price target and it is the amount that you can most expect to make on the trade in question. When you hit a price target you will want to sell off half of your total holdings and move the first stop point up to this point. This maximizes both your profit potential as well as minimizes your total risk.

For example, if you have a pair of options totaling 200 shares of a stock that is worth $20 to start. You would set a stop loss at $19.75 to prevent yourself from losing much money. If the stock then hits your price target of $30, then the best course of action is to sell 100 shares to ensure you see some profit from your price target before holding on to the remaining shares and setting a new stop loss of $30. This way you are guaranteed to see the profits of your previous price target while at the same time leaving yourself open for additional profits assuming the positive trend in the underlying stock continues.

FIND A POINT OF ENTRY

Once you know when you will want to get while the getting is good, you will next want to determine when you are generally going to want to jump in on a profitable options trade. Start by considering your acceptable risk and then decide what you want to do when you find an option that falls within your risk level. The most common entry decision is to buy a single option. Depending on your level of risk, you are also going to want to consider secondary factors, as you want your entry point to be discerning enough to weed out lousy propositions but not so stringent that the good ones also fail to get through. It will get easier to find the perfect entry point, the more practice obtaining trading options.

ASK YOURSELF ABOUT YOUR GOALS

When it comes to creating the type of trading system that is right for you, you must have a clear idea of just what you hope to accomplish when it comes to long term trading so you then have a better idea of how each trade can help you come one small step closer to your goals. You want to keep any limiting factors in mind when it comes to determining your goals, but you also want to keep your goals realistic as well as what is known as SMART.

The best goals are specific in that they make it clear why you want to reach the goal in question as to which requirements stand in the way of your success. It will also make it clear when the goal is likely to be completed, where the completion will take place and who besides yourself you will need to call upon to complete it successfully. Specific goals are important because they are far more likely to be completed than those that are general.

The best goals are measurable which means they have several points that can provide distinct feedback as to the overall success or failure of the goal as a whole. If you know when you have reached a new milestone, then your goal is measurable.

The best goals are attainable when all of your unique challenges are taken into account. No matter your intentions, an unattainable goal is never a good goal.

The best goals are realistic, which means that not only are they attainable, they can be completed based on the amount of time and effort you are able to put forth on average.

The best goals are those which have a specific, but reasonable, timetable for completion. Goals that are too strict when it comes to a timetable will never come to fruition in time; meanwhile, goals that are too vague when it comes to a timetable will also never see success because it is too easy to put them off indefinitely.

KEENLY TRACK YOUR PROGRESS

If you are new to options trading, you will likely find it useful to keep extremely precise notes when it comes to the trades you made, the mental state you were in when you made them, and the outcome of each. Keep track of the metrics throughout your day, every day, but also to avoid pouring over them at the end of each day to pass judgment on your system. A good system needs at least a few weeks to determine if it is at all worthwhile, and then another 2 weeks if its results are near 50 percent or better. Nothing is gained by looking for results where none are strong enough to be accurately seen. Be patient and the information you have to analyze will be much more useful.

PLACE THE FIRST ORDER

Placing your first order is not as difficult as many newbie traders seem to think. All you have to do is obtain the right information and apply yourself. Following are the steps for placing your first order:

LOG IN TO YOUR BROKERAGE ACCOUNT

When you sign up for the services of an online broker, you will be issued a username and password. These are the credentials that will enable you to log in to your account. You must keep them secret. You should even add more security features to keep your account fail-safe. There are many degrees of fraudulent activities on the internet but protecting yourself against these frauds starts with securing your account."

FIND THE TRADE OR ORDER PAGE

It depends on the user interface of various platforms, but since you have opened a trading account, there must be an item on the page labeled "trade" or "order." Brokerages invest in a simple interface so that traders could interact with the options exchange quite easily.

PULL UP A STOCK OR ETF QUOTE

Stocks are the commonest underlying securities that options are based on, so you have to pull the quotes of the company shares that you're targeting.

SEARCH FOR THE OPTIONS QUOTE TABLE

Next up, you have to check the underlying and options price, which are placed conveniently on the search results.

CHOOSE YOUR EXPIRATION DATE

Unlike shares, options have time constraints, so next, you have to select the frame of time within which you will trade, which requires you to set the expiration date of your options contract.

SELECT YOUR STRIKE PRICE

The strike prices for both put options and call options are clearly shown in the table, and you have to select the strike price that you want.

SELECT EITHER "CALL" OR "PUT"

The calls are typically listed on the left side of the page while the puts are listed on the right side. Select the option that you want and check the quotes. The order form for the option will come up.

ENTER THE QUANTITY

Now you have to enter the number of contracts that you wish to purchase. But remember that as a beginner, you have to be careful, which means you have to purchase a relatively small amount of options contracts before you dive in.

SET YOUR DESIRED PRICE

Set the price at which you'll acquire the options contract. The premium is influenced by many aspects, among them, the stock price of the underlying.

PICK OUT THE ORDER TYPE

It is an advanced feature that can help you manage the risk to an extent.

DAY ORDER OR GTC ORDER

At this point, you will decide how long the order will stay open if it's not filled. Day orders stay open during the day and automatically turn off at the close of the market. GTC orders refer to "Good till Canceled Orders," which means they will stay open until they are either filled or canceled.

CONFIRM AND SEND

At the click of a button, your order is placed. Don't rush to do it. Take a moment to review your order to ensure that there are no errors.

Chapter 12

HOW TO CLOSE AN OPEN CALL OR PUT OPTION BEFORE EXPIRATION DATE

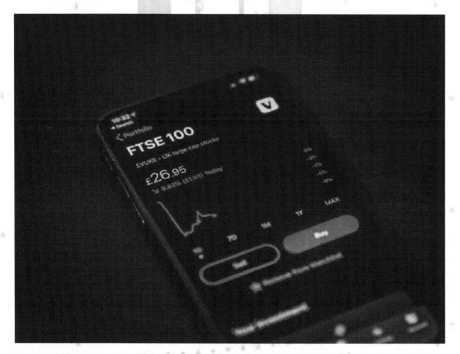

Closing an open call or put option position before the expiration date is similar to short-term trading. Here, you'll make a speculative trade on the assumption that this will pay off.

YOU WAIT FOR SOME TIME AND WATCH THE MARKET CLOSELY

You encounter 2 scenarios:

1. You feel that the trade is in a position to pay you off if you close it now and it might not perform that well by the expiration date. This is your assumption. You can be wrong and may lose on the better payoffs that you might get later on. But you are wise and believe that one in the hand is always better than two in the bush.

You wait for the best strike price at which you will get the highest premium and exit the open position by squaring it off.

2. During the time you have entered into this open position, you have been continuously exposed to the market risk. The trade is not performing well, and you are losing money. You believe that the call option will become zero as it nears the expiration date. Although you are still losing money on the stock you can still get some part of the money by squaring off your position.

YOU CHOOSE TO EXIT THE TRADE RIGHT AWAY, CONTENT WITH THE MONEY YOU GET

Both of these are very probable scenarios. You can either make money on the trade or lose money on it. Exiting at the right time gives you the advantage of getting the benefit of the intrinsic value and time value in the options trade. It is a good strategy if not the best strategy. There is always a chance that the stock may perform quite well in the end. But it is just a chance and there is a strong likelihood the trade might become zero towards the end.

Closing the call option when there is still time to do so before expiry is what we will understand here.

In this strategy, the objective is very clear. The objective is to reap the benefits of the ups and downs in the market.

Now let us understand the way a call option position is squared off.

Suppose you had purchased two lots of call options for ABCL stock at the strike price of $88 with an expiry of March 17, 2019.

Now open your trading portal. There, you'll find all the options you hold. Pick the ABCL call option. In the Actions Menu, you'll find four options to select from.

1. Buy to Open

2. Buy to Close

3. Sell to Open

4. Sell to Close

CLOSING A CALL OPTION

You have bought the call option of ABCL. To close this position, you need to sell this option in the market.

The closing off also works in the same way as purchasing; you can either sell it at the market price or set a rate of yours at which you want to sell your call option.

On the market, the call option will get sold off immediately at whatever the price is available in the market. There is a possibility that you might get a slightly lower rate than you expected. However, the chances are your trade will get sold immediately, depending upon the number of open interests and buyers in the market.

CLOSING A PUT OPTION

It works in the same way for put options. Just open the Action menu after selecting your trade. Now choose the 'Buy to Close' option for closing the put option trade. The remaining things work in pretty much the same manner. You just have to remember that you can only earn profits in a put option if you are selling it at a lower price than you bought it for.

One important thing to remember here is that, apart from the profit and loss, you also have to pay the brokerage of the firm with which you have your trading account. The brokerage is generally fixed on the amount and quantity and it is calculated with the taxes at the end of every trade.

Chapter 13
PLATFORMS AND TOOLS FOR OPTIONS TRADING

A vital aspect of options trading is the platform that one uses to trade. This is because options trading requires monitoring and requires a continuous analysis of trends. Performance is also monitored, and since the trade is impacted upon by a complex of factors, one has to choose a suitable platform for trading.

A good platform for trading should offer a lot of opportunities for traders. These are opportunities to orient beginners into trading, development for the existing ones, and actualization for those with a record on the platform. A platform of trading should also prescribe the available products and any resources that subscribers on the platform can benefit from to push themselves to profitability.

With the technology developing at high speed, platforms continue to improve by the day. This is both complicating the trading itself as well as providing avenues of spreading awareness about the business. A platform should, therefore, have the ability to offer the best possible experience for the traders to do trade and grow both in experience and returns without meeting a lot of platform limitations and frustrations.

Trading involves a lot of complexities that may sometimes be scary. It makes people lose interest as soon as they develop it. They perceive it as too complicated. The impression is that it is a venture meant for the people who have higher comprehension of concepts in the economics specialty and that those who do not have a background in this area will have difficulty getting on board.

However, a trading platform has to present options trading as a venture that is possible and in which anyone with interest can succeed in. The days when options trading and any other forms of trading were presented as a show of sophistication are long gone. In this era, every sector of investment is being portrayed as possible, and businesses are now being made easier to create a better chance for people to dare. A platform that limits investment so much and is exclusive in terms of how it carries out its trading activities is irrelevant to modern economic patterns.

Platforms, therefore, have to be interactive and user-friendly. They should have the ability to encourage users to feel like they can handle the trade. It should also have the capability to gauge the level of use and give feedback about how well they can use it. If it is a website, for instance, it has to be able to report the numbers as people visit it and how many eventually end up creating accounts and trading. Counting traffic is essential for feedback that can lead to the creation of a better experience for the users.

WHY CONSIDER A GOOD PLATFORM?

The reason for considering a good platform is because the competition is high today. Competition has led to the creation of better trading experiences through innovation. Platforms are now trying to out-do each other in being the avenues of options trading. They are doing this by striving to create ways of improving user experience. It is therefore essential to identify the various parameters of comparing the platforms. Eventually, one has to choose a platform that offers optimal access to the trading world.

In choosing a platform sometimes, one would want to take advantage of the advantages of different platforms. This is looking at one's style of trading and how they wish to monitor their business and see if a platform is more transparent in handling the tares or whether it offers a clear lens of controlling purchases and sales of options. This is the reason why the various platforms have to be assessed in terms of their potential. Usually, platforms are related to the tools of trading. Some of the tools of trading can be found right on the platform of trading.

When a platform of trading also has various tools of aiding trading, it ensures that one can gain a lot of benefits in one place. This makes the platform a utility platform where a person can visit for more purposes than just trading. It also makes it better. For instance, if a platform has videos that offer trading tutorials. This can make it resourceful in imparting competency in participating in the very sector that the platform operates.

To best benefit from competition, one has to understand the type of trade they want to do. This is by naming their price and gauging which platform can serve better in ensuring returns and value generation. This is to avoid going into trading in desperation, and one has to be patient to see if the platform can also come out and meet a trader at their point of ability and also help in trading in comfort where risk is at a minimum.

TYPES OF TRADING PLATFORMS

There are various platforms in options trading that one could consider. There is web-based trading that utilizes the power of the search engines. This platform has many operators since the building of websites in the modern age is easy. This platform is responsible for the growth in the popularity of options trading. People can trade from anyone, open brokerage accounts, make deposits, and participate in the buying and selling of assets in the comfort of their homes.

With the presence of a lot of technological gadgets such as smartphones, tablets, and computers, web-based trading has been easy and possible. Websites can be built with additional resources for learning and tools that can be an advantage for both novice and seasoned traders. On the websites, regular updates on the market can be posted to keep traders informed about trends, patterns, and even help in analyzing price movements for the subscribers.

The web is also a good platform when it comes to filtering opportunities and options based on suitability and preference given the various abilities of users. They can be designed to be customizable even when the options markets are standardized.

Usually, websites are good as they offer various tools that aid beginners to edge into trading options. ASX, for example, offers a variety of web-based resources that guide people in their efforts to understand trading. This includes online chats that have instant feedback as a team is dedicated to the work site for correspondence purposes. The aim of this is to offer motivation and impetus to go on with the discovery of the market trends until one becomes a seasoned trader.

Friendliness is also in terms of the efforts that are made to create peer assistance. This is through creating groups of traders that influence each other and can learn from the vast experiences in the trading of the options. This can be a positive influence on the journey to gaining competence and help support an environment where people can relate and interact as they pursue their various financial goals.

You must consider the fact that some of the platforms of trading offer important tools that can help decide on options. The tools are those that help in monitoring markets and simplify the technical analysis process for the trader. This can help one to sharpen their trading strategy to align well with the ultimate goal of trading. This depends on whether the goal of trading is to earn money in terms of profit or hedge oneself against losses on the underlying asset.

OPTION TRADING TOOLS

Upon mastering the various basics of trading and making the initial moves to start trading, one has to use various tools that help to indicate the advancers and decliners on the market. Greeks are some kind of metrics that those involved in options trading capitalize to ensure the maximization of returns. These "Greeks" include the delta matrix that measures the correlation between price movements of the underlying asset relative to the price of the option. The tools for monitoring the movements for these parameters of trading are vital as everyone is always trading with a focus on minimizing losses while geared towards profit maximization.

The gamma is another tool that can help to predict market trends to do good timing for decisions on exercising rights in options. Gamma is an indicator of the rate of delta variations for the option price as compared to the asset price. This goes hand in hand with the time-decay tool that indicators the value movement, either upwards or downwards, in the period of life options. This helps to signal which options to avoid given the remaining time of the life span and the value implications thereon.

Tools are not just concrete things that can be manipulated. Some tools, especially in trading, are conceptual. This is because they are the ones by which one can trade and aid in decision making. They sample out market forces and help in mapping out market trends for the benefit of the trader. To perceive tools as only concrete in nature is a misconception of the whole options trading venture.

PROFESSIONAL LEVEL PLATFORMS

There is a level in trading where one attains sophistication and attains the intuition to thrive in options trading regardless of the ways market forces seem to behave. At this level, someone needs tools that can help them edge into the horizon of complexity in trading. The platforms for this professional level exist, and they have to offer tools that are an edge above the basic level. These tools have to offer strategies of competing to control the stocks and rise above the market forces. At this level, one becomes daring, and the possibilities that the platform offers should only be dared by those who have mastered trading and are sure of beating the odds as they speculate about squeezing out value from trades that otherwise be perceived as highly risky.

The platform should be full of idea probing resources that lead one to gain the courage to trade more and more. Web-based platforms of this level include the think or swim platform that is categorically for seasoned traders. This is the reason why one has to know the platform to trade on based on their level of experience in options trading. Some platforms are too complicated for the starters. The tools are even out of the capacity of a beginner to comprehend the trades appear to have higher risks that may wipe away hard-earned fortunes.

MOBILE TRADING

Mobile trading also comes to keep people abreast. This is because opportunities sometimes appear and disappear on people because they are not using a device that enables them to be precise and timely in decision making and action.

With mobile trading, apps have been developed, some with notification capability. One can customize the apps to ensure that no opportunity comes that is not taken advantage of. Opportunities' in trading have to be seized and relying on a platform that is less handy and far means that opportunities of trading are lost.

SOFTWARE TRADING PLATFORMS

These are more complex than web-based ones. This is because they are run on the trader's computer, and the trader is required to understand what the software does and interpret it. Even when the brokerage can offer assistance, software-based platforms require the trader to have enough technical know-how to read charts, graphs, and understand patterns that represent various components of options trading.

For beginners, a complex platform has to be avoided by all means. This is because one is bound to engage in aspects of trading that they do not have an understanding of. A trading platform simply has to be simple and clear. The interface should not be too busy as to scare away those traders who are not accustomed. This is the reason why operators usually separate the platforms that are designed for basic use, which is suitable for novices, and advanced trading for the seasoned ones.

Then a broker has to offer a tutorial that guides the user on how to navigate their platform. Everything has to be explained, even those that one would deem to be obvious. Screenshots can even be available to be categorical and emphatic. This ensures that a broker has offered all possible assists for the trader to benefit from the offers and products on the platform successfully.

WHAT ARE WE LOOKING FOR IN PLATFORMS AND TOOLS?

First is the opportunity to learn. There is no worse platform of trading than that which targets only to admit traders who do not understand what they are getting into. The education that a platform has to offer should be free as trading is itself risky enough to prohibit any extra expenses in the process. Platform operators should understand that any interested person who visits their platform is a potential subscriber, and they should freely offer support to educate them for the acquisition of requisite knowledge on options trading.

Some of the platforms have gone as opening structures units for education on options trading. These courses are taken online, and coaching is done through the provision of a stream of webinars transmitted live or uploading recorded ones. This is for platforms that appreciate that trading is an informed gamble that requires one to know enough. They even test the proficiency of understanding trading concepts and mechanics to ensure that any people who trade on the platform are doing what they understand to build the platform ratings.

It is also vital for a starter to set standards that the broker's customer service should pass. In trading, brokers should work enough to earn the commission that they charge on the options that subscribers trade on buy. This is because some brokers are obscure and may not involve the options trader who is buying options in decisions that directly impact on his capital. One, therefore, faces a lot of anxiety if the broker is not responsive and transparent on the particular mechanics that influence trade.

Excellent broker services try to suit customer needs. They ask options traders subscribed to their platform what their preferred means of reaching is. Whether a live chat or phone call suits the customer or not. They also dedicate a desk for trading communications and queries and have the discipline to listen to customers and their issues with patience. They have feedback on the quality of customer service that those who reach out get.

The trader needs to know that some brokers may have charges attached to some of the services, resources, and tools that they provide on their platform. These have to be assessed in terms of their worth and whether the costs are necessary. Making some tolls premium may be an indicator of quality but not always. This is particularly the case when other platforms provide similar services toll-free.

Screening tools are particularly the ones that are bound to attract charges because they can analyze and assess market trends. They can think about the trader and help him in decision making. One has to read about the specifications of the tools and ascertain what they or cannot do. This is to know if they are customizable to serve the needs and conveniences of traders.

Some charges can even be attached to the quotes update feed. Usually, the quotes can be accessed in real-time for those who want to see them in real-time. The quotes are important in influencing idea generation and sometimes can tip people of opportunities in the market. There is usually a delay for those who access the quotes updates for free.

It is also vital to understand platforms do not provide all the tools to everyone using their platform to trade. Some of the cutting-edge tools that can best serve the business interests of traders are premium. They have subscription charges or otherwise only appear on the accounts of traders who constantly sustain a certain threshold of account balance minimums. This is particularly the case for platforms that operate at the professional level. They require one to be active and remain active in trading since this serves the business interests of the brokerage through the commissions it earns on options contracts. In return, it offers the consultancy, expertise, and resource repository for one to realize value out of the options trades. This is why they attach a price on some of the tools.

One can only trust a platform that has a reputation for

efficiency. This is a platform that ensures orders have a quick span of execution. This particularly for traders who understand the benefits of entering quickly and instantly exiting from offered positions. The charges of platform subscription also matter. This is whether they are monthly or per year. It is vital to understand the way of earning waivers on platform fees. It could be through ensuring compliance with balance minimums or activity of trades per set period.

172 OPTION TRADING FOR BEGINNERS

Chapter 14
RISK MANAGEMENT IN OPTION TRADING

Money and risk management doesn't get nearly enough attention as it ought to, in my opinion. This is because it's far sexier to talk about fancy strategies and show people how much money they can make. However, risk management is what underlines everything in trading and is what will make sure you keep your money in the long run.

Understand this: It's very easy to make money in the markets. That's right. There's no shortage of traders who make 100% gains per month. Keeping this money is a completely different matter though. Those 100% gains traders usually wipe out after a month or two thanks to the improper risk and money management.

UNDERSTANDING OPTIONS RISKS

The options trading process does carry some risks with it. Understanding these risks and taking mitigating steps will make you not just a better trader but a more profitable one as well. A lot of traders love options trading because of the immense leverage that this kind of trading affords them. Should an investment work out as desired, then the profits are often quite high. With stocks, you can expect returns of between 10%, 15%, or even 20%. However, when it comes to options, profit margins more than 1,000% are very possible.

These kinds of trades are very possible due to the nature and leverage offered by options. A savvy trader realizes that he or she can control an almost equivalent number of shares as a traditional stock investor but at a fraction of the cost. Therefore, when you invest in options, you can spend a tiny amount of money to control a large number of shares. This kind of leverage limits your risks and exposure compared to a stock investor.

As an investor or trader, you should never spend more than 3% to 5% of your funds in any single trade. For instance, if you have $10,000 to invest, you should not spend more than $300 to $500 on any one trade.

Also, as a trader, you are not just mitigating against potential risks but are also looking to take advantage of the leverage. This is also known as gaining a professional trader's edge. While it is crucial to reduce the risk through careful analysis and selection of trades, you should also aim to make huge profits and enjoy big returns on your trades. There will always be some losses, and as a trader, you should get to appreciate this. However, your major goal as a trader should be to ensure that your wins are much, much larger than any losses that you may suffer.

All types of investment opportunities carry a certain level of risk. However, options trading carries a much higher risk of loss. Therefore, ensure that you have a thorough understanding of the risks and always be on the lookout. Also, these kinds of trades are very possible due to the nature and leverage offered by options. A savvy trader realizes that he or she can control an almost equivalent number of shares as a traditional stock investor but at a fraction of the cost. Therefore, when you invest in options, you can spend a tiny amount of money to control a large number of shares. This kind of leverage limits your risks and exposure compared to a stock investor.

TIME IS NOT ON YOUR SIDE

You need to keep in mind that all options have an expiration date and that they do expire in time. When you invest in stocks, time is on your side most of the time. However, things are different when it comes to options. The closer that an option gets to its expiration, the quicker it loses its value and earning potential.

Options deterioration is usually rather rapid, and it accelerates in the last days until expiration. As an investor, ensure that you only invest dollar amounts that you can afford to lose. The good news though is that there are a couple of actions that you can take to get things on your side.

- Trade mostly in options with expiration dates that are within the investment opportunity
- Buy options at or very near the money
- Sell options any time you think volatility is highly-priced
- Buy options when you think that volatility is underpriced

PRICES CAN MOVE PRETTY FAST

Options are highly leveraged financial instruments. Because of this, prices tend to move pretty fast. Options prices can move huge amounts within minutes and sometimes even seconds. This is unlike other stock market instruments like stocks that move in hours and days.

Small movements in the price of a stock can have huge implications on the value of the underlying stock. You need to be vigilant and monitor price movements often. However, you can generate profits without monitoring activity on the markets twenty-four hours a day.

As an investor or trader, you should seek out opportunities where chances of earning a significant profit are immense. The opportunity should be sufficiently robust so that pricing by seconds will be of little concern. In short, search for opportunities that will lead to large profits even when you are not accurate when selling.

When structuring your options, you should ensure that you use the correct strike prices as well as expiration months to cut out most of the risk. You should also consider closing out your trades well before the expiration of options. This way, time value will not dramatically deteriorate.

NAKED SHORT POSITIONS CAN RESULT IN SUBSTANTIAL LOSSES

Anytime that your naked short option presents a high likelihood of substantial and sometimes even unlimited losses. Shorting put naked means selling stock options with no hedging of your position.

When selling a naked short, it simply implies that you are actually selling a call option or even a put option but without securing it using an option position, stock, or cash. It is advisable to sell a put or a call-in combination with other options or with stocks. Remember that whenever you short sell a stock, you are in essence selling borrowed stock. Sooner or later, you will have to return the stock.

Fortunately, with options, there is no borrowing of stock or any other security.

FACTORS WHICH AFFECT RISK

What exactly is risk? Well, to define it at its most basic level, it is simply the probability of you losing your money on a particular trade. Now, the keyword here is probability. Several things affect the probability of your trade being a win or a loss. So, let's look at these and see how you can reduce the risk associated with these individual items.

TECHNICAL STRATEGY

Your technical strategy refers to your entry and exit system in the market. When will you enter and at what level will you exit? Is your entry signal based on sound market principles? This second point is more of a concern for directional strategies since a lot of them tend to be discretionary. With spread trading strategies, as you will see, a lot of this guesswork is taken out of the equation and thus, your risk is automatically lowered.

Exits are something that a lot of traders don't spend a lot of time thinking about. You need to define exactly which levels you will exit the trade at and under what conditions. Then there's the small matter of exiting consistently at profitable levels. It's best to deal with exits as a separate section entirely.

EXITS

With directional strategies, your downside is limited by a stop-loss order, which is just a way of saying 'if the market goes below this level, close out my position.' With spread trading, there is no stop-loss order involved. Instead, we need to focus on the maximum loss amount of a trade.

This maximum loss amount should be a function of our overall account size, expressed as a percentage. Generally speaking, as a beginner trading option spreads, you should not risk more than 1% of your overall account size per trade. This means, if you have an account size of $10,000, you should not lose more than $100 per trade.

Furthermore, you need to keep this risk percentage consistent across every single trade. If you take a loss on your first trade and lose $100, then your overall account size is now $9900 and thus, your new maximum risk per trade is $99. Keep this percentage consistent at all times.

Your average profit percentage should be tied to your per-trade risk percentage, usually a multiple of this. So if you risk 1% per trade, aim to make at least 2% per win, or double your risk every time you win. Now, you don't need to stick to a 2X multiple as a win target. The exact multiple is determined by your win percentage.

Your win percentage is the number of trades you make money on divided by the total number of trades. It is here that most beginners trip themselves up by chasing the highest win percentage. This is understandable since we've been conditioned since our school days to chase the highest percentage of correct answers in any task.

The thing is, the market does not work that way. You can win nine out of ten trades or 999 out of 1000 and still lose money. Think about it: if you lose an amount greater than your wins on that single trade, all of your previous 'correct' answers are for naught. This is why you need to keep your risk percent consistent on every single trade you take.

Your money-making ability is governed by two things, mathematically speaking. Your win percentage and your average win amount. You can have a low win percent but if your average win amount is high enough to eliminate all your losses, then you're making money and it doesn't matter that you didn't get enough answers 'correct'.

Similarly, if you have a higher win percentage then you can afford to have a lower average win amount. The process of determining which average win levels you need to target for a corresponding win percent is something that happens over time. What most traders do is start by targeting a 2X multiple on risk for an average win and after one hundred trades, evaluate to see if they could have pocketed bigger gains and how that would have affected the win percentage.

The key, as ever, is consistency. While it might be easy to take an immediate profit and vow to take a larger one the next time for your average win to remain the same, this is the wrong way to approach things. Ensure your median and mean are the same, statistically speaking. Statistics play an important role in risk management, as we shall see next.

DRAWDOWNS

While your risk per trade and your exits can be controlled by you, your equity curve's direction depends, largely, on the markets. This is because it is possible to do everything right in trading and still lose money. After all, this is why traders need to consider the odds of their strategy and not the certainty with which things might happen.

Your equity curve is the best measure of how well your strategy is playing out, no matter how good or bad it looks on paper. The drawdown is perhaps the most relevant portion of the equity curve. A drawdown refers to a dip in the equity curve. The maximum drawdown is the biggest dip of your equity curve experiences.

You ought to measure the max drawdown both in size (amount), percent of your account equity, as well as time. This last one is important since you will be comparing this time to the time it takes your account to erase this drawdown and make new equity highs again.

This second period is called the recovery period and if it is longer than the drawdown period, your strategy isn't very practical, no matter how much money it makes. This is because, over the long run, you won't end up making much money or will have to wait longer periods to recover your capital, thanks to the slow recovery process your strategy undertakes.

Durability is another aspect you need to consider. While there isn't a fixed number or even measurement to pinpoint durability, you can think of it as a measure of how many trades your system needs to make money on to be successful. For example, a 20% win rate system with an average win of 5X risk is more durable than a 70% win rate system with an average win of 1X risk.

This is because the first system only needs to be correct 20% of the time to make money, whereas the second needs to be right 70% of the time. Also, you can bet that the recovery period of the first system is many multiples faster than the drawdown period.

A lot of professional traders will opt for the first system, while beginners will flock to the second. This, by itself, should make it obvious as to which type of system you should be after. This is not to say that you should design a low win rate and high average win system on purpose. Merely, that chasing after high win rates is missing the point of what trading is about completely.

Your only purpose is to find a combination of a profitable win rate and average win, make sure it has a recovery period that is faster than a drawdown period, and then execute that strategy as many times as possible. The more you execute it, the more money you will make since the odds will play out better.

OTHER MEASUREMENTS

The numbers discussed above are the basic risk numbers you should be tracking at all costs. Beyond this, there are several other statistics such as the maximum adverse excursion, maximum favorable excursion, the sharp ratio, and so on.

These are not particularly important since they're just a reflection of what you're doing in the markets. All of them are a function of the basic measurements I listed above so make sure you are as consistent as possible in your execution and the rest will take care of itself.

Just to make it clear, risking the correct account percent per trade is a part of successful execution. Taking proper exits is a part of the execution. Don't make the mistake of thinking that simply following your entry signal is a successful execution.

FORMS OF RISK

While there are elements of risk that can be measured, there are some forms of risk that are qualitative. This refers to your routines and your preparation before sitting down to trade. How consistent you are with these routines will determine your success in the markets.

PREP ROUTINE

How will you prepare for the market before sitting down to trade? Will you exercise physically? Mentally? Think of yourself as a professional athlete before sitting down to trade. Have you ever seen an athlete change his or her routine before a game? Unlikely. They always go through the same warm-up sequence in a highly structured and organized manner.

You need to do the same before you trade. You cannot expect to roll up after a session at the local bar with your buddies and expect to trade successfully. Neither can you trade hungover or when you're depressed or dealing with some major life situations.

Scheduling some time off from the markets is essential to remaining fresh. A lot of traders get greedy and think they need to remain in the market at all times. This is simply not true. You can execute your strategy only if you're fully fresh and time away from the screen is essential for this. This doubly applies if you have a full-time job, as most readers of this book likely have.

A good idea before sitting to trade is to meditate. Getting physical exercise is also a great way to make sure your mind is fresh. Make sure you've eaten well and keep any other distractions to a minimum. This includes any CNBC or financial channel which is full of useless information anyway.

Remind yourself of why it is you wish to trade and what benefits you expect it to bring if done successfully.

Feel this emotion as you sit down and then begin your analysis of the markets.

Trade at the same time whenever you do decide to trade. This is because the market will have a different dynamic depending on the time of day and the more you're exposed to a particular type of volatility and liquidity, the better it will be for you. So, don't chop and change and sit down whenever you feel like it. This will build inconsistency within you and is bad for your long-term performance.

SESSION ROUTINES

So, you've analyzed the market and have spotted a couple of opportunities that haven't come to fruition as of yet. You'll need to wait for a while before this happens. What will you do in the meantime? Will you browse the internet? Will you finish your errands around your home? Will you stare at the screen like a zombie?

Your task is to stay focused but not obsessively so since this will build fatigue. A good idea is to read a book or something else that keeps your mind engaged but not distracted to the point where you forget about the market and potentially miss your entry point.

Once you enter a trade, what are you going to do? Will you watch over it obsessively, even if it needs no management? Will you count every tick for and against you? Needless to say, this sort of attachment will burn you out within a few days and if you do suffer from this, it points to a lack of understanding of the market's nature.

By thinking that every single trade's result matters, you're ignoring the fact that the odds play out over a series of trades and not just a few. Therefore, you don't need to care about results as long as you execute properly and consistently. Indeed, consistency is what makes money, not fancy strategies.

The point is about focus. Trading calls for a lot of it, even when there's no action around. A lot of trading time is spent sitting around waiting for a good entry. It is only then that there's some activity followed by another long session of doing nothing but monitoring and adjusting. Activity, when it does occur, happens in short bursts and you need to accept the fact that, for the most part, you'll be sitting around doing nothing.

Thus, if excitement is what you're looking for, skydiving might be a better career choice.

POST SESSION ROUTINES

What will you do after the session is finished? Will you review your actions? Or will you take a break and do it later? Do you think you will be able to review your trades if you've experienced a tough session?

It's not possible to answer all of these upfront, but have a plan going in and then be honest with yourself about what you need to do. Generally, I advise reviewing daily as well as weekly. In the beginning, your rate of learning is very high, so you'll be a different trader by the end of the week, thanks to the knowledge you'll be absorbing.

The post-trade or post-session environment is when it's a good idea to reinforce the fact that it is not the individual trade but the consistency of your execution over thousands of trades that will make you money. It is possible to do everything right and still lose money. Indeed, making money on a single trade is simply a matter of luck.

However, over a large number of trades, the odds come into play, and making money over them is a skill. So focus on the longer term and bigger picture. The money will take care of itself.

Hopefully, you can see by now how important consistency is and why this is so. While there are a lot of risk factors you can control over the long run, in the short term you are exposed to the vagaries of the market. There is some risk here as well that you can mitigate; however, by changing the type of orders you place in the market.

This depends on your choice of brokers so let's take a look at this next, along with the regulations and rules you'll need to abide by if you wish to trade options.

RISKS AND THE GREEK LINGO

When it comes to options trading, the various types of risks that come into play are referred to as one of the Greeks. Each variable is then given a different name and there are different ways to go about ensuring that each has as little of an effect on your trades as possible. Trading without first taking the time to clearly understand each of the Greeks and what they mean would be like driving in a foreign country where you were unfamiliar with the basic rules of the road or even the language the signs are written in.

When you look at placing a put or call on a specific underlying stock, or building your general options trading strategy, you must always consider the rewards and risks from three primary areas. The amount of price change, the amount of volatility change, and the relevant amount of time value the option has left. For holders of calls, this risk can further be identified as either price moving in the wrong direction, a decrease in volatility, or there not being enough useful time left on the option in question. On the contrary, sellers face the risk of prices moving in the wrong direction and an increase in volatility but never when it comes to the time value.

When options are combined or traded, you will then want to determine the Greeks related to new results, often referred to as the net Greeks. This will allow you to determine the new difference between risk and reward and act appropriately. Understanding the various Greeks and what they mean will also allow you to tailor your strategy based on your aversion to risk. Consider them as starter guideposts to ensure you are on the right track when it comes to seeking out the right options for you. There are numerous Greeks to consider and each is outlined in detail below:

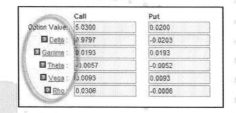

BETA

Beta, β, is a characteristic of the underlying stock and measures the historical volatility of that stock. It gives equal weight to volatility on the upside as well as on the downside. When you are evaluating a stock, you can get a sense of how variable the stock's price is by looking at the β. A stable stock that moves with the market will have a beta value of about 1. If beta is less than 1, it tends to lag the market, that is a $1 movement in the market stock with a beta less than 1 means it will increase or decrease less than $1. Conversely, a stock with a beta greater than 1 means the stock price will move more than the market, up or down. Stocks with low betas are more stable than those with a higher beta. Examples of low beta are utilities. Stocks with a high beta include industries like biotechnology.

DELTA

Delta, δ, measures the change in the price of an option in response to a change in the price of the underlying stock. When it comes to individual options, Delta can be seen as the amount of risk that currently exists that the price of the underlying stock will move. If the strike price of an option is the same as the current price of the underlying stock, then that stock can be said to have a

Delta of .5. This can further be interpreted as meaning that if the underlying stock moves 1 point, the price of the option will shift .5 points assuming everything else remains the same. The total range Delta can be anywhere from -1 to 1. Puts can be anywhere from -1 to 0 and calls can be anywhere from 0 to 1.

Delta is likely the first measurement of risk that you will always want to consider when it comes to choosing the options that are right for you. It becomes beneficial when you want to buy a put option as you want it to be far enough from the current price to make a profit but not so far as to be unreasonable. In this instance, it is beneficial to know the expected results of paying less in exchange for knowing the Delta is lower as well. This difference can be seen by simply looking at the strike price and watching how it changes about the put price.

As a general rule, the less an option costs, the smaller its Delta is. Delta is often linked to the odds that the option will be worth a profit by the time it expires. For example, if you are looking at an option with a Delta of .52, then you can generally assume, all other things being equal, that the option is slightly more likely than 50% to end favorably.

Delta explains the relationship between the change in the cash price of the stock and the change in premium. Delta denotes the proportion in which the change in cash price and premium takes place. If the cash price of a stock rises the premium of the stock option might also increase. But to what extent it will increase is predicted by the Delta.

The formula of Delta is:

Change in Premium/Change in Cash Price

If the price of the stock increases by $10 in the cash market and the premium has increased by $5, then your Delta is 0.5.

The Delta ranges between 0 and 1 in call options. It can be any value like 0.1, 0.2, 0.3, etc.

So if the delta for any call option is 0.3 it means that if the stock increases by $10 then there would be an increase of $3 in the premium.

The Delta for put options is negative. It ranges from 0 to -1.

VEGA

When a position is taken, the risk of change that comes from the volatility of the underlying stock is referred to as the Vega. The level of volatility that an underlying stock has can change even if the price of the stock in question doesn't change; and regardless of the amount it changes, can affect the possibility of profits significantly. The option price is related to the underlying stock price, but the option price is also variable. Vega is a measure of that volatility, but it is implied volatility, not historical volatility as is beta. Vega is the only Greek trading term without a Greek letter symbol. Successful strategies can be built around both low volatility and high volatility as well as neutral volatility in some cases. Long volatility options are those that increase in value as their amount of volatility goes up and short volatility is when value increases as volatility decreases. Strategies or trades that utilize long volatility are said to have a positive Vega and those that use short volatility are said to have a negative Vega. Options that have a neutral level of volatility can be said to have a neutral Vega as well.

As a general rule, the more time standing between an option and its expiration date, the higher that option's Vega is. This is because time value is proportional to volatility as the longer the timeline, the greater the chance of volatility eventually happening will be. For example, if a certain $4 option's underlying stock is currently trading around $90 with a Vega of .1 and a volatility of 20%. If the volatility increases just 1% would be seen by an increase of 10 cents to a total of $4.10. If the volatility had instead decreased, the price of the $4 option would have decreased by 10 cents instead, leaving a total of $3.90. The amount of change that is seen in an option with a shorter period is often going to result in larger changes because there is ultimately less time the option will re-stabilize.

Vega is a measure of volatility in the market. It shows the change in the premium of an option concerning its change in volatility.

This means that for a 1% change in volatility of the option the impact on the option price is reflected by Vega.

Vega = Change in Premium/1% Increase in Volatility

It reflects that the premium would also increase with the same ratio when the volatility in the stock increases by 1%. It is an important Greek to follow when you see any fluctuation in the market. It predicts the change in the premium amount with the change in the prices of the stock.

THETA

Theta: Theta, θ, measures how much value the option will lose every day until expiration. Theta measures the rate at which the time the option has left is disappearing or decaying. This number is frequently going to be negative for your purposes. The moment you purchase an option, your Theta on that option begins decreasing which means the total value of the option begins to decrease as well because options are considered more valuable the longer the period they insure against new risk. The loss is due primarily to the time value of money. As a wasting asset, an option's value will decline because of the concept behind time value. A dollar today is worth more than a dollar next week. This time decay is difficult to calculate and most economic models are complex and often not particularly accurate. If the amount of Delta on an option exceeds the Theta, then the option is considered profitable for the holder. If Theta instead exceeds the Delta, the profits go to the writer.

For example, if an option has a Theta of 0.015 then it is worth 1.5 cents less tomorrow than it is right now. Puts have negative thetas and calls have positive thetas. This is because puts are worth the least when they are about to expire and calls are worth the most because the difference between the starting and ending amounts is at its highest. Additionally, Theta fluctuates day-to-day as it starts slow and then builds in intensity the closer the option gets to its ultimate expiration. This explains why long term options attract buyers and short term options are preferred by sellers.

If you are planning a trade that has the market remaining neutral then you must take Theta into account, but otherwise, it is less likely to play into your strategy. Regardless, aim to purchase an option with the lowest Theta rate as possible.

Theta explains one of the most important aspects of any options trade and that is the time value or the extrinsic value.

We know that as any options trade moves towards the expiration date, the risk involved increases significantly. But we also know that time value is not static for any trade. It keeps fluctuating as per the performance of the stock. It decays all right, but the decay is not steady. The value can increase or decrease suddenly.

Theta explains the risk involved concerning the time decay in the options trade. So, if you have a call option with an expiration date of 90 days you'd want a low Theta risk.

Theta explains to us the change in premium concerning a one-day change in the expiration date.

Some important things to understand about Theta:

Theta will always be negative. It denotes degradation in the value of the premium; hence it can never be positive. It is a value of the time and the time is continuously reducing the options trade. So, Theta will be negative for both call and put options.

It is a Greek that works in favor of the option seller. For the option buyer, the Theta is always a negative attribute. The higher the Theta is the greater the risk of the buyer will be.

It is a very important value. It denotes the degradation of your option with each passing day. It means that, whatever the value of Theta is, it will be deducted from the value of your option trade the next day. The premium will decrease by that amount the next day. If you are considering maintaining your position for the next day in the trade, then you must have a close look at the Theta value. It will give you great insight. You might be expecting a smaller increase in the premium, but the degradation caused by the Theta the very next day might be higher. It is a definite prediction of the loss in value of the premium.

The Theta values are the highest in the ATM trades, the reason for this being that the time value is the highest in the ATM trades and that's why the erosion is also the highest in these trades.

The Theta as an options trade will increase as the trade reaches its expiration.

One of the biggest false assumptions option buyers have is that if the stock keeps increasing the premium will also keep increasing. It doesn't happen this way. The beginners ignore the time erosion caused by the Theta in the value of the premium.

For instance, we take the ABCL stock once again.

The call option stands at $93. The markets are going strong and you have a basis to believe that the stock might rise by a certain value in the next 10 days. But, if you fail to consider the erosion caused by the Theta in the premium then even after the premium rises by those points you will have no gain and might also lose the money in the premium.

Theta will cause mandatory erosion in the value of the options trade with each passing day. The premium will decrease by those many points each day. If the premium is not increasing at a greater pace then you will end up losing money. Napoleon once said, "I can lose a battle but not a minute." The day he lost that minute he had to face the defeat of Waterloo. In the same way, wasting time in an options trade when you do not have any reason to believe that it will rise significantly can prove costly for you.

It's very important to understand the Theta value. It is the definite decay in the value of the premium.

If you are a beginner then you must understand the value of Theta in the trade and always keep it at the back of your mind when forming a strategy. Fooling around and wasting time will cause decay in the premium and you might end up losing money.

GAMMA

If Delta can be thought of as the amount of change that the option will experience when the underlying stock changes, then Gamma can be thought of as the measurement of how the Delta is likely going to change over time. Gamma increases as options near the point where the price of the option and the price of the underlying stock intersect and decreases the further below the strike price the price of the underlying stock drops. Larger Gammas are risky, but they also offer higher returns on average. Gamma is also likely to increase as a specific option nears its ultimate expiration date. This can be taken a step further with the Gamma of the Gamma which considers the rate the Delta changes at.

For example, if a stock is trading at about $50 and a related option is currently going for $2. If it has a delta of .4 as well as a gamma of .1, then, if the stock increases by $1 then the delta will see an increase of 10 percent which is also the gamma amount. If volatility is low, then gamma is high when the option in question is above its strike price and low when it is below it. Gamma tends to stabilize when volatility is high and decreases when it is low.

RHO

Rho is the name for the risk relating to if the interest rates related to the option in question will change before its expiration. When it comes to choosing the system that is right for you Rho will be unlikely to factor into the equation in most instances. As interest rates increase, call prices will do the same while the price of puts will decrease, and the reverse is true when interest rates decrease. Rho values are typically at their peak when the price of the underlying stock crosses the price of the option in question. Likewise, this value is always going to be negative when it comes to puts and positive when it comes to calls. Rho values are more important when it comes to long options and virtually irrelevant for most short options.

FIND THE GREEKS

When it comes to determining Greeks, note that most strategies will have either a negative or a positive value. For example, a positive Vega position will see gains when volatility rises and a negative Delta position will see a decrease when the underlying stock decreases. Keeping an eye on the Greeks and noting how they change is key to options trading success in both the short and the long term.

When it comes to finding the Greeks for any option, the first thing you will want to keep in mind is that the results you get are always going to be theoretical, no matter how good they end up looking. They are simply projections based on a mathematical formula with various variables plugged in when needed. These include the bid you are putting on the option, the asking price, the last price, the volume, and occasionally the interest. This information should then be plugged into the Greek calculator that your platform includes

HOW TO MANAGE RISK IN OPTIONS TRADING

A lot of investors think that trading options is a lot riskier compared to stocks. This can largely be attributed to their lack of understanding of the leverage concept. When applied correctly, options can be just like other securities and not quite as risky. Fortunately, there are ways of working out risks and determining the potential of risk when trading options. It is also a good idea to learn about the power of leverage.

A TRADING PLAN

As a trader, you must come up with a suitable trading plan. Such a plan should be sufficiently detailed and should contain certain parameters and guidelines that outline trading activities. A good plan needs to include detailed information regarding levels of risk that you are willing to take. The plan should also showcase the amount of capital readily available to you.

The idea of using a plan is to ensure that your trades are planned appropriately and that you only trade wisely as you had envisioned. Trading options should not be a gamble, guesswork, or some random trial and error game. Instead, it should be a well-thought-out process with specific funds allocated to specific trades. This way, you will easily avoid most of the mistakes made by those who consider trading options as risky.

Also, when you trade with funds that you cannot afford to lose, then you will be extremely careful about your trading habits. This is one of the ways of limiting risks and introducing discipline to trade. Also, traders who follow a trading plan and stick by it are likely to make informed decisions and will not trade using "scared money."

GETTING RID OF EMOTION

Traders agree that it is not easy to completely get rid of fear and emotion when trading. However, focus is more important. A focused trader with sufficient experience and with a sound trading plan is likely to fare better than a trader with neither experience nor trading plan.

Experienced traders are aware that emotions can lead to the downfall of a trader. Once emotions take over, a trader will toss their trading plan out of the window and start to either recover money that's lost or delay exit from otherwise mature positions. Therefore, greed and fear are the main culprits in this case.

Discipline is the key to successful trading. Traders who focus on studying the markets, conducting technical or fundamental analysis then coming up with a suitable trading plan are bound to be more successful than those who let emotions take charge. Emotions will cause a trade to act irrationally and they will keep throwing good money after bad money. Emotions cause traders to not exit their positions when they have to especially lose-making positions. They believe that a trade will turn around soon and they will recover their lost funds. As such, they keep losing more and more money. Others refuse to exit a winning trade and hang in there risking even the amounts earned. At best traders should exit a winning position, collect profits, and then re-enter the trade.

LEVERAGE

One of the best ways of managing risks when trading options is through the use of leverage. Leverage can be defined as the use of an amount of money to trade at the markets with a significantly larger position than the traditional approach would allow. This is exactly what options traders seek to achieve.

For instance, an option trader with $10,000 can control a much larger stake than a stock trader. This is because an options contract may control about 100 shares at a cost of only $1 per contract while a stock trader will have to pay the full value of the stocks. This is what leverage does. It gives you a huge advantage and enables you to make significantly large profits.

Leverage can also mean controlling a similar stake in the position as a regular stock trader but spending a significantly smaller amount of money. This provides an excellent way for small traders with limited trade capital to invest in the markets with the potential for large profits. A trader's appetite for risk will often determine the kind of trades they enter and the number of funds committed to each trade. Traders should make use of leverage as often as possible if they are to increase their profits exponentially.

Options trading comes with several risks that you need to manage so that you can enjoy the profits and minimize losses.

LOSING MORE THAN WHAT YOU HAVE

This risk is inherent in options trading, especially if you are using leverage to make a trade. It means that you put up a small fraction of the initial deposit to open the trade. This means that your fate is in the hands of the direction of the market. If it goes along with your prediction, you will gain more than the deposit. On the other hand, if the direction changes and you lose the position, you might end up losing more than your initial deposit.

When this happens, you need to have a strategy in place to help mitigate the risk. What you need to do in this case is to set a limit, so that you define the exact level at which the trade should stop so that you don't lose more than you can handle.

POSITIONS CLOSING UNEXPECTEDLY

When positions close unexpectedly, they lead to loss of money. To keep the trades open, you need to have some money in the account. This aspect is called the margin, and if you don't have enough funds to cover the margin, then the position might close.

To mitigate this, you need to keep an eye on the running balances and always add funds as needed.

SUDDEN HUGE LOSSES OR GAINS

The market can turn out to be volatile, and when it does, you need to move fast. Markets change depending on the news or something else in the market, which can be an announcement, event, or changes in trader behavior.

Apart from having stops, you also need to get notifications regarding any upcoming movement, which tells you whether to react or not.

ORDERS FILLED IN ERRONEOUSLY

When you give instructions to a broker to place a trade for you, and the broker instead does the opposite. This is termed slippage. When this happens, use guaranteed stops to make sure you protect yourself against any slippage that might occur.

HOW TO TRADE SMARTER USING LEVERAGE

Even with leverage in tow, you need to have a way to trade better. With many mistakes occurring during a trade, you stand to lose more than gain if you don't have the right tips to excel. Let us look at the top mistakes that you go through to get to the top.

MISUNDERSTANDING LEVERAGE

Many beginners don't understand leverage and go ahead to misuse this feature, barely realizing the risk they are exposing themselves to.

To make this work for you, learn about leverage, and master it. Understand what it is and what it isn't and then find out the best ways to make use of it. You also need to understand how much you can put in without running huge losses.

HAVING NO EXIT PLAN

Just like socks, you need to control your emotions when trading options. It doesn't mean that you have to swallow your greed and fear; rather, you need to have a plan that you can go with. Once you have a plan, you need to stick to it so that even when things aren't going your way, you have something to guide you to make a recovery.

You need to have an exit plan, which means you know when to drop a trade.

FAILURE TO TRY NEW STRATEGIES

You need to make sure you try out a few new strategies depending on the level of trading you want to achieve. Most traders get a single strategy and then stick to it even when it is not working out for them. When this happens, you are often tempted to go against the rules that you set down.

Maintain an open mind so that you can learn new option trading strategies to help you get more out of your trades.

Chapter 15
TOP MISTAKES TO BE AVOIDED BY NEW OPTION TRADERS

BUYING OTM CALL OPTIONS

As anyone might expect, these options are shabby which is as it should be. When you purchase an OTM shabby option, they don't consequently increment because the stock moves the correct way. If the move is near termination and it's insufficient to achieve the strike, the likelihood of the stock proceeding with the move in the now abbreviated period is low. Consequently, the cost of the option will mirror that likelihood.

USING THE SAME STRATEGY IN DIFFERENT CONDITIONS

Option exchanging is strikingly adaptable. It can empower you to trade adequately in a wide range of economic situations. Be that as it may, you can just exploit this adaptability on the off chance that you remain open to adapting new systems.

When you purchase a spread, it is otherwise called a long spread position. Every new options trader ought to acclimate themselves with the potential outcomes of spreads, so you can start to perceive the correct conditions to utilize them.

NO EXIT PLAN PRIOR TO EXPIRATION

You've heard it a million times previously. In exchanging options, much the same as stocks, it's essential to control your feelings. This doesn't mean gulping each dread in a super-human manner. It's significantly more straightforward than that: have an arrangement to work and work your arrangement.

MAKING UP FOR PREVIOUS LOSSES WITH RISK

Every single prepared option trader has been there. Confronting this situation, you're frequently enticed to break a wide range of individual guidelines, essentially to continue exchanging a similar option you began with. Wouldn't it be more pleasant if the whole market wasn't right, not you? As a stock trader, you've presumably heard comparative support for bending over to make up for lost time: on the off chance that you preferred the stock at 80 when you got it, you must love it at 50. It can entice to purchase progressively and bring down the net cost premise on the trade.

TRADING NON-LIQUID OPTIONS

Stock markets are by and large more liquid than their related options markets for a straightforward reason: Stock traders are on the whole exchanging only one stock, however, the option traders may have many option contracts to browse. Stock traders will run to only one type of IBM stock, for instance, yet options traders for IBM have maybe six distinct lapses and plenty of strike costs to look over. More decisions by definition imply the options market will likely not be as liquid as the stock market.

FAILING TO DIVIDEND DATE IN STRATEGY

It pays to monitor profit and profits dates for your hidden stock. For instance, on the off chance that you've sold calls and there's a profit drawing closer, it builds the likelihood you might be allotted early. This is particularly valid if the profit is relied upon to be expansive. That is because option proprietors have no right to a profit. To gather it, the option trader needs to practice the option and purchase the fundamental

FAILING IF YOU ARE ASSIGNED EARLY

For instance, imagine a scenario where you're running a long call spread, and the higher-strike short option is doled out. Starting traders may frenzy and exercise the lower-strike long option with a specific end goal to convey the stock. However, that is presumably not the best choice. It's generally better to offer the long option on the open market, catch the rest of the time premium alongside the option's inborn esteem, and utilize the returns toward buying the stock. At that point, you can convey the stock to the option holder at the higher strike cost.

NOT USING INDEX OPTIONS IN NEUTRAL TRADES

Singular stocks can be very unstable. For instance, if there is major unanticipated news in one specific organization, it may well shake the stock for a couple of days. Then again, even genuine turmoil in a noteworthy organization that is a piece of the S&P 500 presumably wouldn't make that list vary in particular.

SPREAD TRADES

Most starting options traders attempt to leg into a spread by purchasing the option first and offering the second option at a later date. They're endeavoring to bring down the cost by a couple of pennies and it isn't justified regardless of the hazard.

AVERAGING DOWN

Most traders tend to wander across averaging down. It isn't what they had in mind when they first start to trade but end up doing so anyway. Several problems can arise when averaging down. The main thing is that they can lose a position that they are holding on to. This is sacrificing money and time. This money and time could be placed elsewhere that could prove itself to be better.

STRUGGLING TO GET EVEN

If you ever hope to be an expert trader, you need to get used to the idea of being wrong regularly and then work it into your business plan. Letting emotion come into play when you make the wrong bet will only lead you to make additional mistakes down the line. The goal should always be to focus on the cold logic behind the numbers, not a hunt for a way to improve your image or self-esteem. Always focus on price action, leave the worry about magic numbers, and breaking even for when trading is done for the day. The final win/loss ratio can't be tallied until the last trade is made.

UNDER OR OVERSTAYING YOUR WELCOME

Many traders find that they have a good entry plan but a poor exit strategy. This, in turn, leads them to choose a less than ideal time to exit a given trade which leaves them stuck with an investment when they were only looking for a trade. If you find yourself in this scenario you must add detailed technical specifications that will determine when you will exit the trade in question. The specifics of this maneuver will likely change over time and it is common for the strategy to evolve over years, not weeks or months.

GAMBLING

While there is an inherent level of risk in every trade, there is a wide disparity between that and actual gambling. When trading your goal should always be to capitalize on predictive directional signals you have gleaned from checking the statistic, never to bet your money on a hunch. Your goal should be to ensure you remain as disciplined when it comes to making trades as possible. If you are interested in gambling with the stock market, you will likely find better odds for a return on investment in Las Vegas.

MISHANDLING EARLY ASSIGNMENT

Early assignment occurs when a holder exercises an option that you are the writer upon much earlier than you had anticipated, and at terms that are much less favorable than you had initially hoped. If this happens, it can be easy to become flustered and simply sell as requested, taking a loss in the process. Instead, you must consider all the possible options, including purchasing another option for the express purpose of selling it, to ensure that you mitigate the extra costs as completely as possible.

IGNORING THE STATISTICS BEHIND OPTIONS TRADING

One of the biggest mistakes that most newbie options traders make is that they forget that probability is a real thing. When you check a potential stock before purchasing an option, it's important to understand that the history of an option is important when deciding whether or not you should be investing in it, but so are the odds and probability surrounding whether or not a particular event will occur.

BEING OVERZEALOUS

Oftentimes when new options traders finally get their initial plan just right, they become overzealous and start committing to larger trades than they can realistically afford to recover from if things go poorly. You must take it slow when it comes to building your rate of return and never bet more than you can afford to lose. Regardless of how promising a specific trade might seem, there is no risk/reward level at which it is worth considering a loss that will take you out of the game completely for an extended period. Trade reasonably and trade regularly and you will see greater results in the long term guaranteed.

NOT BEING ADAPTABLE

The successful options traders know when to follow their plans, but they also know that no plan will be the right choice, even if early indicators say otherwise. There is a difference between making a point of sticking to a plan and following it blindly and knowing which is which one of the more important indicators of the separation is between options trading success and abject failure. This means you must be aware of when and where experimentation and new ideas are appropriate and when it is best to toe the line and gather more data to make a well-reasoned decision.

IGNORING THE PROBABILITY

Always remember that the historical data will not apply to the current trends in the market at all times which means you will always want to consider the probability as well as the odds that the market behaves the way it typically does. The odds are how likely the market is to behave as expected and the probability is the ratio of the likelihood of a given outcome.

NOT DEALING WITH SHORT OPTIONS PROPERLY

While, in theory, it might seem like buying back short options at the last moment is the best choice, this practice is sure to hurt you more than helping you in the long run. It may be tempting to hold onto profitable options to squeeze the maximum return out of each investment, but you need to be aware that the potential for a reversal is always lurking in the shadows. Instead, a good rule of thumb is to buy back options that are currently at 80 percent of your ideal return or higher and let the extra take care of itself. While it may hurt to leave some potential profit on the table, it will improve your overall reliability, netting you a profit in the long run.

NOT CONSIDERING EXOTIC OPTIONS

An exotic option is one that has a basic structure that differs from either European or American options when it comes to the how and when of how the payout will be provided or how the option relates to the underlying asset in question. Additionally, the number of potential underlying assets is much more varied and can include things like what the weather is like or how much rainfall a given area has experienced. Due to the customization options and the complexity of exotic options, they are only traded over the counter.

BUYING OUT OF THE MONEY CALL OPTIONS

Most options traders adhere to the strategy of buying low and selling high. However, when you buy out of the money calls, you hurt your chances of making a profit, and when the losing streak becomes prolonged, it could render your trading strategy unproductive. Those highly susceptible to this mistake are the traders who operate on a small budget.

GIVING IN TO FEAR AND GREED

Options trading requires a trader to be very forward-thinking and in charge of their emotions. But traders don't always exercise their emotional intelligence. For instance, when a trade is winning, an investor might get greedy and resist closing their position, simply because they want to allow the trade more time to go even further up. Greed can also manifest when an options trader is adamant although they are losing consistently. When losses become your constant companion, it's time to pull out and reevaluate your strategies. If you're executing appropriate trading strategies, there's no reason you should struggle to make a profit. Traders who are driven by fear tend to overreact to every small thing that goes wrong. For instance, they bail out at the first sign of incurring a loss.

DOING POOR ALLOCATION

Never commit more than 5% of your portfolio to one options trade. As much as options have leverage and high earning potential, you cannot ignore the high level of risk exposure. Thus, you have to allocate prudently.

HAVING A FINITE APPROACH

Options are flexible and can work with almost any securities market. But a single trading strategy doesn't achieve the same results across all securities markets. If an underlying asset is hardly moving, an out of the money call or put option is likely to expire worthlessly. However, taking covered options can be profitable in this scenario. Iron Condor, a trading strategy that involves taking many positions, would generate a profit if the underlying moves slowly.

NOT HAVING AN EXIT PLAN

Before you start trading, you should fully understand what you're trying to get into. How much money do you intend to make? What are your risk-reduction measures? Once you have answered the critical questions, you will be in a position to make appropriate strategies and learn how to exit with the least possible scars when you're losing money.

IGNORING CONSISTENT PROFITS IN FAVOR OF HOME RUNS

Options traders tend to forgo the chance of making small yet consistent amounts of profits and focus their energies on nailing the elusive home run. If you have a trading strategy that seems to net you small but consistent earnings, you should stick to that.

HAVING A STRATEGY THAT DOESN'T MATCH YOUR OUTLOOK

An options trader is supposed to have an outlook of what they expect to happen. Technical analysis and fundamental analysis play a part in developing your outlook. Technical analysis promotes the interpretation of the market's volume and price on a chart, whereas fundamental analysis is mostly about reviewing a company's performance data. Thus, a trader must always take the trading strategy that marries their outlook.

ATTEMPTING TO RECOVER PAST LOSSES

A trade can move against you and make you lose money. Most traders have been there. Sometimes you may put your capital on options, and the outcome is not exactly what you expected. In such a scenario, most traders tend to double up their options strategy to see if they can recover the loss. Doubling may lower your potential for loss in a given trade, but it is surrounded by a lot of risks.

TRADING IN ILLIQUID OPTIONS

Liquidity in options trading refers to having active sellers and buyers on the market all the time. This is what drives competition. It also affects ask and bid prices for options and stocks. The stock market is often more liquid than the options market because stock traders focus on one commodity, while options traders often have several contracts to select from. An option quote always has the bid price and the asking price indicated on it. These prices do not indicate the actual value of the option. Illiquidity in options trading may result from illiquid stock. It is therefore important to trade options that are derived from a highly liquid stock.

Chapter 16
TIPS TO HELP YOU SUCCEED WITH OPTIONS TRADING

START WITH ENOUGH CAPITAL

You should always leave a little bit of money in your trading account. This will help you out when you are in the middle of a trade and can make it easier for your broker to keep working on trades without having to worry about a delay while your funds transfer. The most successful traders in options will always check their accounts and make sure that they keep enough capital there so that even if there are a few bad trades along the way, they still have that nice cushion to rely on to help them.

AVOID THE REALLY BIG RISKS

It is true in investing that the higher the risk, the higher the reward. This may be the way to invest for some people, but for the average trader, it will spell disaster. If you want to be able to say that you are profitable with options trading, then you need to make sure that you keep your risks to a minimum as much as possible.

TRADE AT THE RIGHT TIMES

Since you will learn how to avoid big risks when you are an options trader, you will learn how to be very careful about your timing when it comes to entering and exiting the market. You have to be able to read the market the right way so that you can learn the best time to do both of those tasks. These investors have spent their time doing some research and they know how to look at the big picture, rather than always calling up the broker and hoping that they can trust that person.

COME UP WITH YOUR PLAN

You also need to make sure that you are picking out a plan that is unique to you and that has things that you are willing to follow. While there is nothing wrong with listening to some experts in the field and considering what they say, it is never a good idea to just follow exactly what they say without considering it or thinking it through. What works for someone else may not completely work for you so think things through before you just jump right in.

LEARN HOW TO BE FOCUSED

Some of the most successful traders on the market are the ones who can keep themselves focused on the task at hand. There are quite a few people who have an idea that options trading is super easy and then they jump in and become overwhelmed by what they are dealing with. If you are not used to this kind of investment, it may seem a bit hard to deal with in the beginning.

NEVER FOLLOW THE CROWD

One of the worst things that you can do is try to follow the crowd and hope that will work out well for you. Many beginners find it easy to look to the experts for advice and then they will follow exactly what that expert says without doing any of their research or trusting their judgment. There is nothing wrong with getting advice from an expert, but your plan will not be the same as theirs. You are the only one who has an idea of your limits and your goals and while you can listen to the advice that others give you, you must think for yourself and pick out a plan that works for you.

REMAIN ON TOP

Remember to take advantage of the tremendous assets of the Internet and buy into the many investment opportunities trading pamphlets, join forums, and remain over options trading news. Make it a day by day propensity to read up on what's happening in the market.

COURSES AND TUTORIALS

A standout amongst the ideal approaches to begin your raid into trading is to get yourself a course, system, or exploit a few tutorials. There are many basic tutorials available for nothing on the web that will give you the basics of investment opportunities and trading with them. Many tutorials even have recordings, models, and other intelligent components that can be entirely crucial to somebody new to purchasing with investment opportunities. There are likewise various courses that are available on the web and disconnected, many incorporate electronic books, memberships, forums, recordings, DVDs, sound documents, spreadsheets, and different materials. A course that is intended to teach you how to trade can be essential to a beginner to options trading.

PROGRAMMING

At long last, there are various options with regards to options trading programming. These product bundles and systems can enable you to mimic and examine situations and can be essential instruments in your investment opportunities trading weapons store.

UNDERSTAND TECHNICAL AND FUNDAMENTAL ANALYSIS

Before you start trading, ensure that you carry out an analysis of the market. Technical analysis involves the study of how the price is expected to change. The idea behind this concept is that you can study historical patterns in price changes and determine how the price may change in the future.

Fundamental analysis, on the other hand, helps you to analyze social, economic, and political factors that may affect the demand and supply of the stock you wish to trade-in. Supply and demand affect the price change and can be used to detect the direction of stock prices easily. In a nutshell, technical, and fundamental analysis of the market helps you to identify similar patterns around the price and make informed decisions on your options.

HAVE ENOUGH CAPITAL

The reason why most beginners do not make it in options trading is not having enough capital. Most people get excited at how easy options trading can be and think that they can make an instant profit from their little capital in a matter of days. However, before they realize it, a few trades have swallowed their capital. They are then left with nothing to trade on. To be on the safe side, start with a good amount of cash that can sustain you for several trades.

GET A SUITABLE TRADING STYLE

What differentiates traders is their preferences, personalities, and trading styles. You need to understand the style that suits you best. For example, some traders prefer working at night, while others are more effective in day trading. Some of the traders will make several short sales during the day while others will factor in the issue of time and volatility just to gain a large profit over periods that may last between a few days and a month.

BACK-TEST YOUR TRADING STRATEGY

Back-testing is a very important aspect when it comes to developing a winning plan. It entails evaluating your existing strategy and style against the market history to see how best you will perform. Although past performance does not necessarily determine future success, doing this will give you a rough picture of how your strategy and style may perform at different times and setups. In case you are unable to do this by yourself, you may engage a software company or Forex broker to do the back-testing for you.

CREATE A RISK MANAGEMENT PLAN

Having a plan is vital for your success. You need to have it in place before you start trading. Remember, options are high-risk tools, and you must have strategies in place that can help you minimize the risks involved with each trade. Use your money wisely. Diversify the stocks you trade in to reduce the potential of losing all your capital. Most of the expert traders only seal a contract when there is low risk and high profits.

BE PATIENT AND DISCIPLINED

Patience will help you get the right opportunity to make a profit. Expert traders can stay idle for days, just watching the market and waiting for a good time to make or close a sale. Impatient traders will always complain of less profit or huge losses. Wait for the odds to work in your favor and focus on the bigger picture. Patience and discipline will help you stick to your capital and risk management plans. These attributes also assist you to avoid trades you are not successful in.

UNDERSTAND THE MARKET CYCLE

The options trading market keeps changing every time. You need to remain updated on the market trends and make the necessary adjustments to your plan accordingly. Through constant learning, you will be able to learn new strategies and identify better trading opportunities that other traders bypass.

KEEP RECORDS

Having a record of your past trades can help you determine when to make a call or put option successfully. Some of the successful traders keep records of all their transactions. Analyzing these records continuously can help you identify vital patterns in the options you are trading in. It can also help improve your odds in the trade.

STUDY THE CHART

Before you make any trade, there's one thing you must always do, and I mean always. You need to look at the chart of the underlying stock and study it well. This is done to find trends, patterns, resistances, etc. So, you study the one-month chart first, then the three-month chart, and then for the whole year. You will be able to see whether there are any trends in the chart.

TRADE ROBOTICALLY

Being a successful trader means being able to react at a moment's notice, without hesitation, full stop. The only way you can ever ensure that this is the case is if you can put aside the emotional aspect of what is occurring and focus on the numbers as if it was some else's money. A good way to ensure that this is possible is to make it a point of never putting more on the line then you can afford to lose.

DON'T ALWAYS FOLLOW THE CROWD

While doing what the major players in the market do can be a reliable strategy, following the crowd at all times is not advisable in the long-term. Successful traders do their research and trust themselves enough to act on the results they determine, even if they mean making trades that might seem unpopular at the moment. When it comes to seeking substantial payouts trading against the market is the most likely, if not the most reliable, option. This is only the case if you do so for the right reasons, however, as being a contrarian just for the fun of it isn't going to get you any either.

BE CONSISTENT

Before you ever make any trade, you will want to have a clear idea of the strengths and weaknesses of the various stocks in question as well as the best point to enter into a trade and at what point you will want to exit the trade if things go poorly, and also where you will exit if things ultimately go as well as you could expect. Once you have made a plan you must stick with it even if your emotions are making a compelling argument for going in another direction instead. You must always trust in your plan as it was made during a period when you were thinking as rationally as possible, giving in to your emotions at this point is akin to gambling with your investments.

KEEP THE MOOD OF THE MARKET IN MIND AT ALL TIMES

Fundamental and technical analysis is all well and good, but they will only take you so far before you run into instances where the market seems to balk at the logical choice and move off in an unexpected direction. This typically happens when the will of the market goes against the status quo thanks to an unexpected outpouring of support from traders who are thinking with their guts instead of their brains. The best way to go about doing this is to keep tabs on what the major players in your market of choice are up to as this will typically act as a litmus test when it comes to the feelings of the market as a whole.

KEEP A TRADING JOURNAL

To get the most out of this process you will want to keep track of each trade you make along with the date, the state of the market and the underlying asset that you were basing all of your trades on, whether the trade ended up being profitable or not and your emotional and mental state while you were trading.

BE WARY OF OVERTRADING

Keep in mind that, even if you are already steering clear of truly terrible trades, the odds are high that you are still trading far more frequently than the pros. What's more, if most professional traders traded as frequently as the average amateur then they would like to be out on the street after a week. Generally speaking, aim to limit your trading costs to less than two percent of your total portfolio to ensure that your returns remain as high as possible.

AVOID OUT OF THE MONEY OPTIONS

While many investment markets focus on buying low and selling high, the simple fact of the matter is that this doesn't work when it comes to options trading. Putting any of your trading capital towards a call option that is out of the money is a little better than gambling and there are far more effective ways to gamble if that is what you are looking to do. Furthermore, making these types of trades can also make it difficult for you to understand just why the trade failed in the first place, meaning you can't even learn from your mistakes.

LEARN WHEN TO USE VARYING STRATEGIES

When it comes to trading in the options market successfully, there are countless different strategies to choose from which means you have no excuse when it comes to attempting to fit a square peg into a round hole. For example, if you decide to buy on spread, this could be an excellent way of capitalizing on some very profitable market conditions, but only if you know the specifics before you get started. Not only will focusing on a single strategy cost you money regularly, but it will also skew your overall results with that strategy as it will include countless false losses that could have been turned around if you had been using the right tool for the job.

HAVE A CLEAR IDEA FOR EVERY ENTRY AND EXIT POINT

To ensure you can eventually turn a profit in the options market, you must always have a clear idea of both what your entry and exit points are. Failing to do so will make it difficult to mitigate the influence your emotion might otherwise have on your trade. It will also serve to ensure that you remain in the black over the long term. While it can be difficult to exit a trade when there is still the potential of money on the table, you must keep in mind that the potential for loss is also ever-present. Setting a reasonable exit point and sticking with it will generate a larger profit over a prolonged period, guaranteed.

NEVER DOUBLE UP

If you are in the midst of a trade that is going your way, only to have it turn on you at the very last minute, it can only be natural to want to do everything in your power to save it. Unfortunately, the best option practically every single time is to simply cut your losses and move on. Never forget, options are derivatives which means that the price is likely to change with little notice which means that doubling down is only going to end up ultimately costing you more in the long run.

STAY AWAY FROM ILLIQUID OPTIONS

Illiquidity measures the speed at which a specific option can be either bought or sold without causing the price to shift noticeably. Liquidity, on the other hand, can be thought of as a chance that the second round of trading for a given underlying asset will end up taking place at a price that is close to the same price as the first round.

DON'T BUY BACK SHORT OPTIONS

While, theoretically, it could seem like buying back short options at the last moment is an ideal choice, the fact of the matter is almost always going to hurt you more than helping you in the long run. Additionally, it may be tempting to hold onto profitable options to squeeze the maximum return out of each investment, but you need to be aware that the potential for a reversal is always lurking in the shadows. Instead, a good rule of thumb is to buy back options that are currently at 80% of your ideal return or higher and let the extra take care of itself. While it may hurt to leave some potential profit on the table, it will improve your overall reliability, netting you a profit in the long run.

NEVER MAKE A TRADE YOU CAN'T AFFORD TO LOSE

When it comes to deciding on how much you will spend on your new options adventure, you must keep in mind that you should never invest more than you can afford to lose. If you decide to invest money that you need for more pressing matters in a volatile market, then you will never be able to look at your trades rationally and will always be concerned about protecting those funds. It is also important to factor in how long you anticipate holding the options for as the more time you have, the more you will be able to let loose and take risks as you will have plenty of time to correct them if things don't work out.

AVOID DISCOUNTING VOLATILITY

Being aware of the amount of volatility that is currently plaguing a specific market is crucial when it comes to making positive trades that will end up paying out in your favor in both the short and the long term. Understanding the current level of volatility in the market of your choice is quite simple as all you need to do is consider the stock market as the volatility of all the other markets is likely to reflect the same level of volatility as it does at least 9 times out of 10. The greater the degree of stability that the stock market is experiencing the more confident the majority of traders are across the board which means the overall level of stability will more or less remain the same.

DON'T OVERCOMMIT

While sticking with a single asset makes sense when you are learning the ropes of options trading, sticking with one underlying asset for too long can severely curtail your profit potential. As such, once you feel comfortable trading options it is best to start looking into multiple different assets to ensure that if one segment of the market unexpectedly turns sour that you don't lose all of the trading capital in one fell swoop. Remember, there is plenty of uncertainty in even the calmest markets as uncertainty is what leads to profit as far as investment is concerned.

BUY CHEAP OPTIONS

Sometimes it is hard to know what the cost of an option is but generally, always try to buy cheap options. Mostly, try and buy options at no more than $1. However, if it is a blue-chip stock, then ensure that you stand to gain leverage at least 25 times or more. This means if the stock price is $50, then do not pay more than $2 for the options.

FIND A MENTOR

When you are looking to go from casual trader to someone who trades successfully on the regular, there is only so much you can learn by yourself before you need a truly objective eye to ensure you are proceeding appropriately. This person can either be someone you know in real life, or it can take the form of one or more people online. The point is you need to find another person or two who you can bounce ideas off of and whose experience you can benefit from. Options trading doesn't need to be a solitary activity; take advantage of any community you can find.

KNOWLEDGE IS THE KEY

Without some type of information that you can use to assess your trades, you are playing at the roulette table. Even poker players show up to the table with a game plan. They can adapt to the circumstances and learn to read other players. That way, they can tell the contenders from the pretenders. Options trading is no different. If you are unable to use the information that is out there to your advantage, then what you will end up with is a series of guesses which may or may not play out. Based purely on the law of averages you have a 50/50 chance of making money. That may not seem like bad odds, but a string of poor decisions will leave you in the poor house in no time.

OPTION TRADING FOR BEGINNERS

Conclusion

Thank you for making it through to the end of this book, the next step is to find a suitable broker and start practicing your skills. It is only through regular practice that you will be able to hone your trading skills.

After reading this book, you must have figured out how easy options trading is. With the information covered here plus your desire to make it in options trading, you have no option but to excel in the business. You are now better prepared to trade options using technical analysis, fundamental analysis, and other procedures. You are also ready to take opportunities as they come and have a sense of what each trade entails, from a technical view.

You should also work out your best strategy and stick with it. If you have managed to identify a good strategy, then that is great. If not, then take a look at a couple of strategies and try and discover which one suits you the best.

Trading can be a very lucrative process especially options trading. However, you should apply everything that you have learned to prevent losses. You do not want to clean out your trading funds. Therefore, start small and progress with caution until you gain sufficient confidence to make bigger purchases.

There is so much potential for making a profit when you work in options, but you have to come up with a plan and stick with it if you want a chance for success. This guidebook will help you to reach that success so that you can limit your risks and make as much money as possible with options.

Try and build your confidence this way and then move to an online trade simulator. Here, you will trade just like you would on a broker's platform. However, you will use virtual money.

It is only after you are thoroughly versed with options trading, including common terminology, trading strategies, and so on that, you can now sign up with a broker and open a trading account. If you follow the instructions in this book, then you will begin making good profits in no time. Options are very lucrative and can make you wealthy if applied well. Good luck in your trading career!

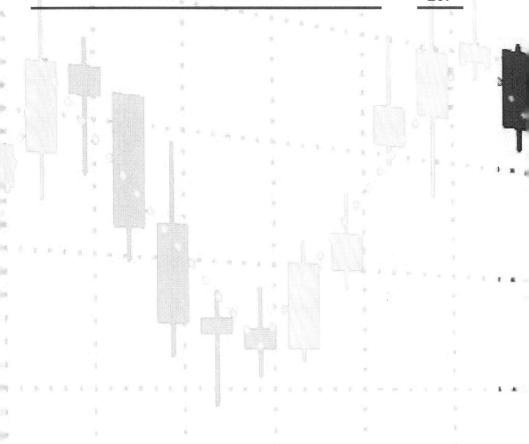

Made in the USA
Columbia, SC
05 November 2020